D0838873

MONEY,
THE ROOT OF ALL HAPPINESS
PETER·M·CLEVELAND

GAI·GARET
design &
publication ltd.

Published by
Gai-Garet Design & Publication Ltd.
Box 424
Carp, Ontario, Canada K0A 1L0
(613) 839-2915

ISBN 0-921165-09-9
Printed and bound in Canada
©1990 by Peter M. Cleveland

Art Direction by Wendelina O'Keefe
Cover illustration by Ray Knowles
Text illustrations by Sean Darragh
Typesetting by EpiSet Electronic Publishing

Canadian Cataloguing in Publication Data
Cleveland, Peter M
    Money, the root of all happiness

Includes bibliographical references.
ISBN 0-921165-09-9

    1. Money – Humor.   I. Title

PN6231.M66C43 1990   332.4'0207   C90-090201-9

Dedicated to
My Partners
and
the staff of Ernst & Young

Acknowledgements

Special thanks to my secretary, Ms. Mary Conway, and to Paul Kavanagh for all their efforts, dedication and patience necessary to complete *Money, The Root of All Happiness*.

Money, The Root of All Happiness

Table of Contents

Forewarning

Money, The Root of All Happiness is meant to be a fun look at the history of money, to reveal its effect upon our lives and provide a peek at its potential future role. Most books written on the subject of money have revolved around how to make it, make it grow, or how to spend it. It is the author's opinion that there is more humour and fun to money than it has been given credit for by most previous authors. Consequently, the time has come to place this commodity in its proper perspective.

$ $ $ $ $ $ $

There are many hopes and dreams, anxieties and suspicions surrounding the concept of money and all it has stood for throughout the years. Like man, it has built a history for itself, and as such, it has suffered, prospered or advanced in the esteem in which it has been held throughout the years.

History has provided money with the ultimate in power over man, substantially through the motivation of his behaviour. The two are so closely associated that it is not possible to study the history of man, or even evaluate his current and expected future behaviour, without tendering the same courtesy to the history of money. Yet, at the same time, one cannot help but feel that the power of money has been taken so seriously throughout history that its material worth, in terms of what it may acquire, has greatly undershadowed the true spirit of its own ascent. Therefore, there is an overwhelming need for *Money, The Root of All Happiness,* to overcompensate for such an historical imbalance of facts.

To effectively correct this imbalance, it is, of course, necessary first to review, and then take inventory of, the history of man
and his money. And, as there is no better place to begin than the
beginning, one is forced to refer to the oldest history book in the
modern world – *The Bible*.

From *The Bible* will emanate the beginning, development and
evolution of the effect of money upon the life of man. The evolution
will not always be clearly visible in the mind of the reader, but then
neither is money. Therefore, those who read on will, from time to
time, be required to rely heavily upon the word of the author.
Although certain events and facts may not have happened just as
they are written in *Money, The Root of all Happiness,* they ought to
have happened in such a way, and for this reason the author has
emotionally and intellectually accepted any deviation from reality
with indifference. It is now up to those who read this book to
demonstrate the same level of maturity.

With respect to the historical environment within which
money has resided, altruisms have been explored to the point of
distortion, and this will delight those who feel money has always
resulted in distortion. But people must be cautioned, out of fairness,
that distortion may not always be negative. Such is especially true
when money has been deployed to distort unhappiness through
delight. Those delighted at the distorted effects of money may
become so by thinking delight is distortion in the first place.

In the case of the future, of course, one is less certain of the role
of money. Notwithstanding this obvious fact, there is no reason
why the distortion of facts and events of the past could not be used
to project the same for the future. Indeed, it may be easier to use
such past events to preview the future, especially since the future
has not yet produced any of its own reliable documentation. Hence,
to establish an appropriate level of credibility for the future of
money, *Money the Root of all Happiness* has chosen to view it in
the past.

Prologue

Li Sum looked out over Tokyo Bay from the balcony of his high rise condominium. With hands clasped behind his back he stood and contemplated his long, rich and rewarding life. "Such an odd thing, money," he mumbled. "One spends one's entire life accumulating it – but to what end? Perhaps it is to be faced with the difficult task of explaining it to one's grandson."

In 2050 this was a very difficult assignment indeed. "How do I package the history of money, the manner in which it has moulded human nature and, in turn, how human nature has created the current economic world?" Ever present in Li Sum's mind these days were the words of his grandson, Sum Yen: "There is so much for me to learn about money, Grandfather – where it came from, how negotiations began and when businesses were developed. Can you recount the history of money for me, Grandfather?"

So, perplexing as it was, this was to be the undertaking of Li Sum; to prepare a history of money for Sum Yen. "I must begin immediately," whispered Li Sum to himself...

1

Biblical *Barter* – Part I

In the beginning, there was no money.

God was unhappy because he had no method by which to measure the non-progress which was taking place. He was bored, having plateaued in his ecclesiastical position. There were no pressures, no problems and, therefore, no thrill in the position of the supreme being.

So God created the universe as the first step to grief and misery and, hence, potential job satisfaction for Him.

He said "Let there be light" – and light appeared.[1] God was pleased so He separated light from darkness. Light, He named day, and darkness He named night.

At the time, God did not realize light and darkness were as different as day and night. But He did realize that from the first day anything He created would be considered good and have an association with brightness, or light. Things not created by Him would be considered dark, undesirable and eventually unacceptable. Light was to represent the increase in wealth and the hope for humanity. Darkness was to represent a decrease in wealth and the presence of evil. It was helpful, in a way, that this matter was clarified on day one.

The next day, God commanded "Let there be a dome to divide the water and to keep it in two separate places" – and it was done.[2] He named the dome "sky".[3] And "blue sky" would represent optimistic and potentially unreasonable financial expectations in life. It would be construed by man to represent endless desire, hope

[1] Genesis, Chapter 1, Verse 3
[2] Genesis, Chapter 1, Verses 6–7
[3] Genesis, Chapter 1, Verse 8

and greed. But not to God! It's funny He didn't see the light of day, given that this was the second one in history.

Then God commanded "Let the water below the sky come together in one place, so that the land will appear" – and it was done. He named the land "earth", and the water which had come together he named "sea".[4] Earth was to be created as solid ground, and the sea was to be something in which to sink. Now the groundwork had been laid for the accumulation of wealth and a place designated, for those who did not take heed, to sink financially.

On the third day, God commanded, "Let the earth produce all kinds of plants, those that bear grain and those that bear fruit" – and it was done.[5] The third day was very fruitful. The earth now had two commodities upon which to speculate, harvest and sell – two commodities which ultimately would have to be measured by something.

Then God commanded, "Let lights appear in the sky to separate day from night and to show the time when days, years, and religious festivals begin; they will shine in the sky to give light to the earth" – and it was done.[6] So God made the two larger lights, the sun to rule over the day and the moon to rule over the night; He also made the stars. All of this He completed on the fourth day. This seemed to be a strange sequence of events since one would have required the sun and the moon to tell when the first, second and third days ended!

Nevertheless, one now had an atmosphere in which to create more things of different value for the purpose of understanding relativity. But the world did not yet know whether night and day had any relationship with the eventual creation of money, and hence, whether money would be acquired in a different manner during darkness than light.

On the fifth day, God commanded, "Let the water be filled with many kinds of living beings, and let the air be filled with birds." So, God created the great sea-monsters, all kinds of creatures that live in the water and all kinds of birds.[7] The birds and monsters were to feed on something and some things were to feed on them. This created the law of supply and demand – as creatures were always in demand of each other. Then God commanded,

---

[4] Genesis, Chapter 1, Verses 9–11
[5] Genesis, Chapter 1, Verse 11
[6] Genesis, Chapter 1, Verses 14–16
[7] Genesis, Chapter 1, Verses 20–21

"Let the earth produce all kinds of animal life: domestic and wild, large and small" – and it was done.[8]

And then God said, "And now we will make human beings; they will be like us and resemble us. They will have power over the fish, the birds, and all animals domestic and wild, large and small."[9] He blessed the human beings, created them male and female and said, "Have many children, so that your descendants will live all over the earth and bring it under their control. I am putting you in charge of the fish, the birds, and all the wild animals. I have provided all kinds of grain and all kinds of fruit for you to eat; but for all the wild animals and for all the birds I have provided grass and leafy plants for food" – and it was done.[10] God was pleased with what He had done during this sixth day.

During this sixth day, man was made the superior physical being on earth with the awesome responsibility of being in charge of all that had been created. But much had been overlooked here! How was man to account for all this responsibility? What medium was he to use to take inventory of his charge? Such a medium had not been created, and so, one is forced to take issue with the conclusion that the whole universe was completed on the seventh day. Indeed, the job had not been completed as air, light, darkness, plants, monsters and human beings had no history of co-existence and, hence, no means to measure any equilibrium among themselves. What was the balance of nature and how was one to tell when its components were in equilibrium?

After all, such equilibrium had to include some method of measuring value – but this was not taken into account by history during the first six days of earth. After all, there was really nothing to value nor anyone yet to make value judgements. And, since the seventh day was one of rest, the concept was given no further consideration at the time.

$ $ $ $ $ $

The newly created human being as well as the beautiful fruit trees, clear water and plants were placed East of Eden. In the middle of the garden stood a tree which was to give life and a tree to give knowledge of what was good and what was bad. God's plan was to

---

[8] Genesis, Chapter 1, Verse 24
[9] Genesis, Chapter 1, Verse 26
[10] Genesis, Chapter 1, Verses 28–30

teach man a lesson in this garden. So Adam, the name the first man gave himself, was told by God he could have any fruit in the garden except that which came from the tree that gives knowledge of what is good and what is bad.

God said, "You must not eat the fruit of that tree; if you do, you will die the same day."[11]

When Adam was asleep God took out one of his ribs and formed woman. She was named woman because she came from man. But the creation of woman from man made her second in history, and since this beginning, no woman has been content with this position. Resentment of second place by woman ultimately sowed the seeds of the feminist movement. And so her creation brought into being not only man's first companion but also his ultimate nightmare.

This first woman was named Eve and wasted no time in providing both pleasure and destruction in Adam's life.

A snake said to Eve, "Did God really tell you not to eat the fruit from any tree in the garden?"

"We may eat the fruit of any tree in the garden," the woman answered, "except the tree in the middle of it. God told us not to eat the fruit of that tree or even touch it; if we do, we will die."[12]

The snake replied, "That's not true; you will not die. God said that because he knows that when you eat it you will be like God and know what is good and what is bad."[13]

So Eve ate the fruit and gave some to Adam and when they ate the fruit they immediately discovered they were naked and so they used fig leaves to cover themselves. They tried to reason this discovery and its relationship to fruit, but the knowledge once acquired made them believe naked was an ugly concept. So that day, they really had exposed themselves to the good, the bad and the ugly all from eating the forbidden fruit. They could only conclude they were to stay away from all fruits while naked.

God was not happy with this and punished the snake by making him crawl and slither on his belly for ever. Moreover, his name was assigned for all eternity to those who attempted to deceive others for personal gain. All those who engage in trickery to acquire and accumulate wealth, overlooked by God in the first place, were "snakes". They were the symbol for all evil, and any symbol of evil or temptation God referred to as the "devil".

---

[11] Genesis, Chapter 2, Verse 17
[12] Genesis, Chapter 3, Verses 1–3
[13] Genesis, Chapter 3, Verses 4–5

God said to Eve, "I will increase your trouble in pregnancy and your pain in giving birth. In spite of this, you will still have desire for your husband, yet you will be subject to him."[14] Women, for thousands of years, have referred to portions of this biological punishment as "the curse".

And to Adam, God said, "You listened to your wife and ate the fruit which I told you not to eat. Because of what you have done, the ground will be under a curse. You will have to work hard all your life to make it produce enough food for you. It will produce weeds and thorns, and you will have to eat wild plants. You will have to work hard and sweat to make the soil produce anything, until you go back to the soil from which you were formed. You were made from soil, and you will become soil again."[15]

Now God thought justice had been done. But as a final step, He sent Adam and Eve from the Garden of Eden to provide for themselves. Eve was outraged at the harshness of this and promised to turn over a new leaf. She thought all this seemed fairly harsh for the time because before there had been no harshness with which to compare the punishment. As a matter of fact, there were many things which hadn't existed before, but because God laid down his creative tools on the seventh day, man and woman were not provided with all things necessary to anticipate what was yet to be developed. The one thing that had been made clear was confusion because:

- no one trusted a snake;
- man would never listen to his wife again;
- woman would always blame man for "the curse"; and
- man would always blame woman for having to work.

And of course, one cannot forget that God had created the devil.

But what had all this to do with money or a medium of exchange? Virtually nothing except that good, bad, evil, punishment and distrust had been placed somewhat into perspective. All bore some cost in life. All required a price to be paid and all inspired certain motivation and behaviour. But at this point, what was cost or price? There was no association of these concepts with anything nor could there have been at the time. After all, the ink was not yet dry on the map of the world, and the warranty had not expired on the universe. Consequently, one was still missing

---

[14] Genesis, Chapter 3, Verse 16
[15] Genesis, Chapter 3, Verses 17–19

certain key ingredients before man was driven to develop the concept of money.

So by laying down His creative tools on the seventh day, God left man without any accountable medium of exchange – an historical fact which was bound to lead to economic turmoil in future years. Had He anticipated this, God would, in all likelihood, have worked one more day. However, the fact that He did not, later helped man to understand that a fortune could be won or lost in a day.

$$\$ \$ \$ \$ \$ \$ \$$$

One did not have to wait long before additional key ingredients, necessary for the founding of a medium of exchange, appeared.

Adam and Eve gave birth to two sons, Cain and Abel. Cain became a farmer and Abel became a shepherd. And after some time, Cain brought some of his harvest as an offering to God. Similarly, Abel presented God with the first lamb born to one of his sheep. God was pleased with Abel's offering but not with Cain's.

Now this did not seem to be a fair approach because, after all, these were the only two offerings God had received to date. One normally would have been thankful for both. But, more importantly, by showing pleasure for one offering over another, God blessed relative value, a concept which was already acknowledged as not having been created during the first six days of the universe. By choosing the gift of one over another, God introduced the characteristics of competition and jealousy between Cain and Abel. Cain could not cope with this feeling because a medium of exchange did not yet exist to make obvious the fact that a lamb was worth more than food by soil. He ultimately was driven mad with anger and killed Abel. God decided to punish Cain by driving him from the land.

In the absence of a medium to measure the already blessed relative value, Cain killed Abel for no measurable personal gain. And since he was banished by God, Cain would never be able.

$$\$ \$ \$ \$ \$ \$ \$$$

Cain ultimately married and sired children who, in turn, sired many descendants along with the other children of Adam. These descendants amounted to no more than a quart of oil each, and that was only after they had been dead for two thousand years!

The only descendant of Adam who impressed God was Noah. The interesting thing about Noah was that he did not have his three sons until he was five hundred years old – terrific stamina!

During Noah's lifetime, mankind spread all over the world, and girls were born. The girls were looked upon as beautiful and were sought after by man. The attraction of man for woman lead to promiscuity and prostitution, and then to violence from those men who didn't acquire the first two.

And because of these evil thoughts and deeds, God said, "I will not allow people to live for ever; they are mortal. From now on they will live no longer than a hundred and twenty years."[16] He regretted that He had made everyone on earth because of how wicked they had become. The violence and prostitution was too much. And so, He was filled with sorrow and decided to rid the earth of all but Noah. The great flood was to follow.

Through Noah an opportunity existed to begin life a second time and to eliminate wickedness.

So violence was used to negate violence, which at the time seemed to be an acceptable form of wickedness – a school of thought later developed throughout the history of man's behaviour concerning wealth. Wealth, once discovered, eventually assumed the role of rationalizing what constitutes accepted wickedness.

$ $ $ $ $ $

After the great flood which destroyed all living things on earth, Noah released the animals God ordered him to protect on the ark. The animals, as well as Noah, his wife, their three sons and their wives, reproduced to create the descendants who repopulated the earth. Reproduction was the main theme for the next several thousand years, but it is a topic not considered socially acceptable to discuss here in any detail.

One of the descendants of Noah was Abram who later changed his name to Abraham. Now God took a liking to old Abraham just as He had to his forefather, Noah. This was an important fact because Abraham was aware of the history of man and the oversights in the creation thereof. He knew this from family discussions among the descendents of Noah.

During Abraham's time, God once again became disgusted with the existence of wickedness, particularly in Sodom and Gomorrah. And again it was His first inclination to destroy these

[16] Genesis, Chapter 6, Verses 1–3

Abraham invents negotiation with God by haggling over the destruction of Sodom and Gomorrah

cities. Abraham said to God He could not do this because innocent people would be punished along with the guilty. Abraham asked if there were fifty innocent people, would God kill them? God said He would not. What if there were forty-five innocent people? But God said He would not destroy the cities if there were forty-five innocent people. They continued to haggle and Abraham negotiated God down to ten innocent people. If ten such people existed, the cities would not be destroyed. This was the first negotiation ever to have taken place. Hence, Abraham was credited with the invention of negotiation – a tremendous accomplishment when one considers his opponent!

Although God agreed to negotiate, sulphur still rained upon the cities of Sodom and Gomorrah, killing all except a man named Lot and his two daughters. So both the first negotiated and reneged deal had been experienced at once, all while God was choosing a different lot in life. But still there was no money with which to measure the loss experienced by the cities of Sodom and Gomorrah.

Even old Lot got screwed! His two daughters felt sorry for themselves as there were now no men to father their children – only

Lot survived. So they got him drunk and each slept with him, resulting in each giving birth to a male child. The children, of course, could not distinguish their father from their grandfather, but that made the family situation economical when it came to giving gifts. One of the sons was the founder of the tribe of Moabites, and the other of the Ammonites. Although both sons suffered severe intellectual deficiency due to inbreeding, they went on to become union leaders during the years when the pyramids were being built. Obviously, in certain instances, the wrong lot was chosen!

Genesis, or the beginning, devoted the balance of its story to sex, sin and travel. When one stops to think, priorities have not changed much since man's first few years on earth.

The descendants settled over the earth in places which ultimately bore their name. Many travelled and settled in Egypt following the holy man, Joseph, who died there at the age of one hundred and ten.

But, to continue the pursuit of the founding of money, one must turn one's thoughts to *Exodus*. Before doing so, however, one must take stock of the key ingredients, created to date, which eventually influenced the development and use of money. By the time Egypt was well established, man had developed the following personal traits:

- competition
- jealousy
- the ability to kill
- revenge
- promiscuity
- evil
- negotiation
- the ability to renege on an agreement
- anger, and
- in-breeding

All these behavioural patterns were learned from the relatively newly created devil. But man's learned wickedness had not yet been influenced by money. Nevertheless, the existence of such behaviour was to be fundamental to the founding of money as a medium of exchange. So now that wickedness had been defined, the world was waiting for some value to be placed upon it.

$ $ $ $ $ $ $

The Israelites were cruelly treated in Egypt when they were taken into slavery. So, as the Israelites became stronger in numbers, the King of Egypt felt threatened and, to control the population, ordered the firstborn son of every Hebrew family thrown into the Nile.

At this time, two Hebrew children of the same name, but different families, were born. The first Moses was born of the Levi tribe – a tribe whose descendants dedicated themselves to the design and creation of clothes. The second Moses was born of the Moullah tribe – a tribe whose descendents were dedicated to the creation of economic chaos. The two babies survived the Egyptian raids for firstborn males and grew to become friends.

Moses of Levi was a nationalist and was greatly troubled by the slavery of his people. He was poor but followed God faithfully as he was called to do.

Moses of Moullah became a camel trader initially until he could decide what to do with his life. Now the trading of camels was looked down upon during these times as it was considered the lazy man's way out of working in the fields to feed his family. Notwithstanding this, there was a substantial demand for used camels in Egypt because not many people could afford to raise their own herd. Moses of Moullah's business, therefore, appealed to the un-herd of!

Now, Moses of Moullah quickly got into trouble with his business when he tried to exchange two camels where one was in better health than the other. This presented some difficulty for his regular customers. After many unpleasant encounters, he chiselled a note from stone which promised to account for the difference in health, strength or value between one camel and another. Because it was a promise on a note, he called it a *promissory note*.

At first, a customer who received the weaker camel plus one of Moses' promissory notes was reluctant to accept such an arrangement. But since Moses of Moullah was the only camel trader in the land, the market forces of supply and demand pressured the trading public into accepting the promissory notes. And to be fair, Moses always honoured these notes when the customer returned for camels in the future. So Moses of Moullah's promissory notes not only gained acceptability but also trust among Jews and Arabs alike – even though not many Jews and Arabs were alike.

Moses of Moullah casts money in stone for all time by becoming the first chiseller of promissory notes

Now Moses' regular customers were always in possession of some of these promissory notes. They became known as *moullah* because they were only as good as Moses of Moullah's word that they would be accepted as part-payment for the next camel trade. Moses' credibility spread, by word of mouth, far into the land as people heard of *moullah*.

Once, a foreign camel trader named Barticus was travelling through the land of Canaan when he found himself without food. He stopped a man in Jericho to ask for food, but the man would not spare any for Barticus. He asked, "What am I to receive in return?"

"I have nothing of value," said Barticus.

"You have a camel, don't you?" said the stranger.

"Yes, but if I give you the camel in exchange for food, I will not be able to continue my journey," said Barticus.

"But I need a camel and you need food," proclaimed the stranger.

"Well," said Barticus, "I do have these promissory notes which are called *moullah* in the city of Rameses."

"Ah, I have heard of this man Moses of Moullah," said the stranger, "and I will soon be travelling to Rameses! Because of the

Barticus founded barter when he offered moullah notes *in exchange for food*

great honesty of this man of Moullah, I will accept a *moullah promissory note* in exchange for some food. I shall do this only if the note will buy me a camel when I journey to Rameses."

Barticus was amazed when *moullah* notes helped him acquire items other than camels. So he gave the stranger four notes which was the amount required to purchase a camel from Moses. He took some food from the man and continued on his journey.

Now Barticus was shrewd, and since he had a sufficient number of camels for his own needs, he decided he could better his lot by using *moullah* to negotiate many other things. The years saw him become a fierce negotiator and acquire as many goods as possible in exchange for as few *moullah* notes as possible. Abraham would have been proud of him. But because of his tenacious approach, people began to distrust him. Barticus was mocked in Bene Jakaan and all those who attempted to adopt his mercantile business style were chided as "Barterers", a then sarcastic derivation of his name.

Throughout the years to follow, though, the soundness and trust in the integrity of Moses of Moullah and his notes remained intact. No matter what *barter* took place as a result of Barticus' business practices, Moses always honoured his promissory notes distributed throughout the land.

In the beginning, Moses was puzzled as to why someone would take the notes for something other than a camel. But since he was profiting by the exchange of more camels, it really didn't seem to matter.

In the course of this widespread use of promissory notes, Moses found himself losing track of how much *moullah* was held by the people and how many camels he should have on hand at any one time. To solve this problem he decided to keep an inventory of *moullah* just as he did with his camels. In order to accurately scribe the promissory notes he had to number them. This lead to a greater mystery – not all the notes were being returned to Moses for the purchase of camels! People were using them to buy other goods, and those who were selling other things, in turn, used the notes to purchase for their other needs. In many cases these promissory notes changed hands in perpetuity, became lost, or were destroyed over the years.

The interesting thing about this whole process was that Moses became the wealthiest man in the land because not all the promissory notes were presented to him for credit. That is, he distributed his notes by purchasing goods and services for his own needs but also kept most of his camel herd intact. So he didn't really become rich from camel trading, he become rich from notes which everyone trusted could be exchanged for something else! *Moullah*, or its slang term money, became the world's first medium of exchange!

A medium of exchange had now been founded as something to exchange to reflect value. And whatever the people used as a current medium of exchange was referred to as *currency*. The national exchange of any one currency would become an economy – a name given to the affect of multiple exchanges upon the lives of a nation of people.

Now Moses was no fool. He wasn't going to spend his last eight hundred years cleaning up after camels with note paper when he could really use camels to clean up on the note paper which everyone thought had a magic power to acquire things. Once he discovered the magic of the notes, Moses chiselled more than could be supported by his camel herd. And he did this on the assumption that only a small portion of the *moullah* would ever be presented to

Enlargement of the crude moullah note - *the first medium of exchange*

him in return for camels. As in the past. the surplus *moullah* was used to acquire additional goods and services for himself. It never occurred to Moses that the power of this note developed and existed only because people believed in him – that *moullah* could always be presented to him in exchange for a camel. He did not realize he had created *the camel-backed currency* (The CBC), and that if people lost confidence in this CBC, it could be disastrous for the land.

$ $ $ $ $ $ $

During the many years to follow, *moullah* developed into an international currency, all while Moses of Levi was tending flock in Midian. He was deeply troubled by the slavery of his people, and God spoke to him, concerning the matter, from a burning bush. God told Moses he was to accept the responsibility of leading the Israelites out of Egypt.

Moses met with the King of Egypt many times, and each time the King promised to let the Israelites go into the desert to pray and make sacrifices to their God. But each time he reneged on his promise. So God empowered Moses to deliver a message of displeasure to the King through punishment of the Egyptians – there was the stick which He turned into a snake, the Nile turning to blood, frogs over-running the land, the gnats, the flies, the death of the animals, the boils, the hail and the locusts. But the King was so stubborn he withstood all, and couldn't wait to see what was to happen next.

God then informed Moses that the firstborn male child of every Egyptian home would be killed during a given night. He instructed Moses to have all the Israelites celebrate this as the first Passover, and God said this would be the last punishment he would deliver to the Egyptians.

Moses knew this punishment would be more than the Egyptian could bear, and they would drive the Israelites out, perhaps even kill them in the process. So he knew his people would have to leave the country quickly, and that he must prepare them immediately.

One of his major concerns was how to finance the moving of an entire nation. He knew of no one else to turn to but his boyhood friend who had become the nation's most successful merchant – Moses of Moullah.

So Moses of Levi met secretly with Moses of Moullah and told him of all that had happened, and what God was to do next. Moullah looked at his old friend in wonder and then stared pensively at the ceiling for some time.

"Well," he said, "I do have the financial resources to move six thousand men, women and children. But if what you say is true, Moses, there will be chaos. The Egyptians will blame everyone. Confidence will be lost in the Government, there will be looting and killing! With all this, my *moullah* will become worthless because its strength is built upon calm and the orderly conduct of business. In the absence of such order, people will lose confidence in me and there will be a run on my camels – that is, a financial run. The economy of the country and my fortunes will be destroyed. Furthermore, when people discover I, the owner of the promissory notes, do not possess enough camels to satisfy all the notes, I will be killed – no mercy will be shown."

"Then," said Moses of Levi, "you are a wealthy man only between now and the time God takes the life of the firstborn male of every Egyptian family. You, Moullah, have one last chance to put your wealth to a good purpose."

The two schemed through the night and the next day Moses of Moullah went to see the King.

"You have been visited many times by Moses of Levi who has requested you to release God's people," proclaimed Moullah to the King.

"Yes, but I have chosen not to let the chosen leave for it would be at great cost to me," replied the King.

"But to worship our God in our own way is important to our people," argued Moullah. "Can we not barter like you have done many times with Barticus?"

"What do you have to secure and protect me from the loss of six thousand slaves if they choose not to return?" queried the King.

"I will assign to you all my *moullah* and all my camels as security for the slaves," said Moullah triumphantly. "If the people do not return from the desert where they will worship their God for three days, my wealth is yours. If the Israelites do return, then my wealth shall be returned to me. Is it agreed?" demanded Moullah.

"It is agreed," said the King, "if you sign over all your wealth to me now."

So the agreement was made and all the *moullah* was left with the King. Moses of Moullah and Moses of Levi spread the news that the King was now the owner of the *moullah* promissory notes as well as all the camels to back the currency. No one was to believe that Moses of Moullah was in control of the wealth from that day forward.

That night the firstborn male of all Egyptian families, including the King's son, was killed by God. As Moses of Moullah had predicted, rioting and chaos followed. The King was in such a rage that he threatened to kill every Hebrew in the city. But instead, he contained himself with the thought of holding all Moullah's wealth. This wealth would afford him the opportunity to profit from ridding his people of the Israelites. So the King spared the Hebrews their lives but banished them from the land.

Moses and Moullah quickly moved their people before the King discovered what had really taken place. The Israelites were moved out of Egypt in three days – at the same time thousands of Egyptians stormed the King's palace demanding camels in place of their *moullah*. The King could not understand why the people were so enraged at him and not the Hebrews. When his advisors explained that the people had a claim against Moullah for all their

The first economy collapses in a sea of red

moullah, the King realized he had been tricked and been made to look the court fool. He was beset with rage once again, and ordered all his legions to hunt down the Israelites.

When the people discovered their *moullah* no longer had a trading value they felt cheated. And because the King held all the camels and promissory notes, and Moses Moullah had never cheated them, they could only blame the King. Two days later, while the King's men were searching for the Hebrews, the King was caught and stoned to death by his own erstwhile loyal subjects.

$ $ $ $ $ $ $

Before his death, the King ordered his war chariots and his army ready for the Hebrew pursuit. His officers set out with six hundred of his finest warriors, and all the King's horses and all the King's men caught up with the Israelites on the shores of the Red Sea. ·

God said to Moses, "Lift up your stick and hold it out over the sea. The water will divide, and the Israelites will be able to walk through the sea on dry ground. I will make the Egyptians so stubborn that they will go in after them, and I will gain honour by my victory over the King, his army, his chariots, and his drivers. When I defeat them, the Egyptians will know that I am the Lord."[17]

So Moses held out his stick over the sea and the Lord drove the sea back with a strong East wind. It blew all night and turned the sea into dry land. The water was divided and the Israelites went through on dry ground, with walls of water on both sides – just as God had predicted. The Egyptians went after them into the Red Sea but God made their chariot wheels mire in the mud to frustrate their crossing.

The Lord said to Moses, "Hold out your hand over the sea, and the water will come back over the Egyptians and their chariots and drivers."[18] And the Egyptians drowned in the Sea of Red on the same day the King was stoned to death for his inability to back the *moullah* promissory notes, thereby collapsing the world's first money, currency and economy – all in one day! From that day forward, to be without money, to have lost money or to be in debt was to be in "the red". "A Sea of Red" would become a term to describe the financial status of a person, entity or country having insufficient money, currency or monetary backing to pay his or its debts.

$ $ $ $ $ $

The Israelites continued on their journey to Mount Sinai. When they arrived, Moses made a number of treks to the top of the mountain seeking advice and direction from God. At first God ordered Moses to tell the people to believe only in Him for all time. Moses came down and told the people, who said they would follow God. Moses went back up the mountain and God told him to go down and order the people to cleanse themselves for worship and the people said they would do everything the Lord commanded. So Moses reported this to God. But Moses was becoming tired of this shuttle diplomacy between God and the people; however, God would not permit anyone else to come near.

The last climb up Mount Sinai saw Moses of Levi gone for a long period of time. The people were scared, and although God had forbidden the creation of false material gods, they turned to Aaron to make them a god to worship.

Aaron went to Moses of Moullah for advice because of the great respect Moullah had earned when he gave up his wealth for the Israelites. Moses Moullah told Aaron to gather together all the

---

[17] Exodus, Chapter 14, Verses 16–18
[18] Exodus, Chapter 14, Verse 26

gold and jewelry from the people which Aaron did, without question.

Now Moses of Moullah was a clever man. He knew the people possessed a desperate need to believe in something. And he was still bitter about the loss of all his wealth. So his need to replace lost wealth and the people's need to have faith in something presented an opportunity – one which would permit the creation of an idol as a symbol of wealth.

And so it was done. All the gold and silver was melted into the form of a calf – a sacred calf. Everyone worshipped the sacred calf and brought sacrifices to it from which Moses of Moullah profited. Since he built the calf, everyone was content to have him as chief caretaker – or the one who organized sacrifices and worshipping. After all, it was a small sacrifice for him to make!

Moullah told the people the golden calf wished him to chisel new *moullah* promissory notes to be issued to them. They were to purchase things once again – pleasurable things to make them happy. And because the people could once again enjoy pleasurable things, they abandoned their true faith to *worship the golden calf* which became a cash cow for Moses Moullah. The people brought food and staples as sacrifices to the sacred calf, and, since Moullah was the caretaker, he received the food in the name of the golden calf – then, he subsequently sold it back to the people for them to eat and make further sacrifices in exchange for *moullah.*

Moses of Moullah was excited at all this because the golden calf replaced his first CBC. In fact, the idol did more than become a new currency backing because its power of worship kept the people from realizing that Moses of Moullah was backing a new economy with the people's new religion – all in one!

Since all new promissory notes issued by Moses Moullah had the blessing of the sacred calf, the notes became *"calf-backed currency"* or The CBC. But because the original currency was *"camel-backed currency"* and also called The CBC, the golden calf-backed currency then became "The CBC II". Any historical reference to the first currency, henceforth, became The CBC I.

Now The CBC II was much more popular than The CBC I because no one would ever stoop to worship a live camel under the CBC I. Although it may have been physically possible to do so, it was certainly not considered a pleasurable objective from a worship viewpoint.

Moses of Moullah gathered his new wealth in a short period of time and in amounts which far exceeded that which he had lost when he left Egypt. And the people were happy with an abundance of food and drink and their continuous orgies. The new *moullah* promissory notes certainly brought happiness – at least for the time being.

After some time on Mount Sinai scribing all the laws and the basic Ten Commandments God wished to project, Moses of Levi went down the mountain to tell the people of their new way of life. When Moses saw what had occurred in his absence, he was furious. The people were dancing, drinking and worshipping gold between orgies. And no one could understand why, with a lifestyle such as that, Moses would be so upset.

He threw down the tablets, upon which God inscribed The Ten Commandments, on the sacred calf. The tablets broke. And Moses melted the calf, ground the remains into powder and made all the people drink it with water. This created confusion among the people because they had now consumed a portion of what they considered to be a temple. Did this mean that their bodies were now temples?

Moses of Moullah was not confused. His body was now a temple of doom! The CBC II had been destroyed, and so, Moullah became the first richest man on earth for the second time – only to be the first man reduced to poverty twice. In both cases, Moses of Levi, his best friend, had been instrumental in the cause. He began to suspect that his best friend was a socialist – a conclusion with which he could not live.

Then Moses of Levi replaced the sacred calf by building "The Tent Of The Lords' Presence"[19]. He used all the camels to haul wood and straw from afar. Moullah's last camel was used for this project and as it brought in the last load of straw, it was so heavy and had been carried for such a long distance the camel's back was fractured. For Moses of Moullah, this was the straw that broke the camel's back! He could tolerate no more failure and left immediately for the promised land.

$$\$\ \$\ \$\ \$\ \$\ \$\ \$$$

The effects which Moses of Moullah had upon the people of Israel did not go unnoticed by God. Among the many laws He had set down for Moses of Levi were those pertaining to currency

---

[19] Exodus, Chapter 26

transactions. For example, loans to the poor were to be made interest-free. And no profit was to be taken on food sold to them. However, everyone was poor during this time so the law had the affect of preventing all from earning a profit. Consequently, everyone remained poor. And because no one progressed, no one was happy – no one except God who had laid down certain laws for payments to be made to Him under certain conditions.

God told Moses that when a person gave or devoted himself to God, that person could only be set free by payment of a *tithe*. God set the following official standard for such tithes:

"- adult male, twenty to sixty years old: 50 pieces of silver

– adult female: 30 pieces of silver

– young male, five to twenty years old: 20 pieces of silver

– young female: 10 pieces of silver

– infant male under five: 5 pieces of silver

– infant female: 3 pieces of silver

– male above sixty years of age: 15 pieces of silver

– female above sixty: 10 pieces of silver"[20]

It would appear that all were not of equal value in the eyes of the law makers! By these standard tithes, prejudice against the young, the old and the female population was introduced. It was the beginning of the concept of self-worth and inferiority complexes.

People were forced to seek silver from the ground in order to meet their tithes to God. If they could not locate such silver they were to present animal offerings in lieu thereof. The local priest was responsible for fixing the equivalent value of the animal in terms of silver. And, of course, the priests had no learned method to do so, other than the exchange or currency system founded twice by Moses of Moullah.

Now, what did all this really mean? Well, Moses of Levi was used to destroy the financial empire of Moses of Moullah on two occasions. Then, when all the laws concerning tithes were set down, it became clear that the priests were attempting to monopolize all profit for themselves. With Moullah out of the way the priests set laws against generating profits from the poor, and then created taxation of the poor for themselves – all of which made *moullah* profits look like *chicken feed*. The poor became poorer and the priests became richer. As this became clear to man, the stage was set for a continuous battle for wealth between the priests who

---

[20] Leviticus, Chapter 27, Verses 3–7

wished to accumulate it in God's name, and man who wished to control it through *moullah.*

The tithes had begun with taxation on the land – and that was where the priests received their greatest profit in God's name. They preached throughout the land that God was lord of the land – or the first landlord.

The priests became corrupt throughout the years collecting more and more tithes in the name of God. The people longed for Moullah and prayed for his return. The people complained to the priests and when they did they were told that God wished them to be punished. And after their punishment they were to leave and cross Jordan into the land of Canaan – this was to be the promised land. They were to drive out the inhabitants of that land. And it was done for all but one – Moses of Moullah.

$ $ $ $ $ $ $

By the time the Israelites had found Moses of Moullah, God had instructed Moses of Levi to pick his successor. In so doing, Moses chose Joshua to lead the Israelites upon his death. This was to be with the help of Joshua's brother, Como. But, Joshua and Como were schemers and the people did not hold the same faith in them as they did in Moses of Levi. However, they were the chosen because they would stop at nothing to eliminate any possible competition for the priests' tithes and taxes. But what the two successors to Moses had not counted on was that Moullah was a very able competitor for wealth, and that he had secured help to do so.

During the three years Moullah was separated from the Israelites, he acquired vast amounts of fertile land, and his produce and fruit crops had flourished. When Joshua and Como arrived in the promised land, they learned of this success and were concerned it would affect the tithes paid to the priests; so they spoke with Moullah.

"You must not compete with the Lord in acquiring great wealth," they said.

"This I cannot promise," replied Moullah. "I have such a reputation to uphold. And in any case, you must take up the matter with my business partner who is in a land far from here. He shall not return for forty days and forty nights."

"And who might your business partner be?" queried Joshua.

"A man from a distant land who answers to the name of Barticus," replied Moullah.

Joshua and Como looked at one another and realized at once they had been had by the priests. They now realized they were sent to the promised land to oppose the priests' competition from both Moullah and Barticus at the same time. They remembered what a fierce negotiator Barticus was and what he had accomplished with the original *moullah* notes. The founder of barter and the founder of the first currency were now together in the name of profit at a time when all other Israelites were expecting a prophet!

Moullah had never forgotten the joy and pleasure his first two currencies had brought him. And with his reputation still intact in the promised land, he was determined to achieve financial success once again. But, this time he had acquired a skill which was missing from previous attempts – that was the skill of negotiation now available to him through his partner, Barticus.

Together, Moullah and Barticus devised a plan which saw a division of their duties based upon their skills. Moullah created new notes and oversaw the land while Barticus negotiated the purchase of seed with the promissory notes and sold the produce and fruit back to the suppliers at the standard value, plus twenty per cent. These prices were set to be competitive with the priests and, in the absence of any price fixing laws set by God, this was an acceptable practice to all except the priests. And so Moullah and Barticus prospered greatly at the expense of the priests. Now Moullah knew he could not refer to his new notes as *moullah* as long as he was forced to maintain a low profile among the priests. Since Joshua and Como were under great pressure from the priests to arrest him, he thought a code name was necessary for the notes. But the code had to be totally unrelated to either his own name or that of Barticus.

Now, coincidentally, with this image problem, Moullah's mother-in-law, Moonie, went mad and had to be placed in shackles. He did not want anyone to associate madness with him anymore than with the name of the new notes. This ruled out the possibility of naming the notes *mad moonies* or *mad money* as it was pronounced to accommodate the laws of slang. No. He needed something more obscure than that to link the two problems. He had to restrain himself just as Moonie had to be restrained by shackles. That was it! He would name the notes shackles to denote the fact that both he and his mother-in-law were forced, albeit in different ways, to maintain a low profile. And, the name was even more appropriate than Moullah realized because the people's ability to carry out business was also restricted by the number of shackles they possessed.

Shackles grew in number and acceptability throughout the promised land. They replaced silver pieces as a material with which to exchange goods and services, and to value one item against another. This annoyed the priests further because they found themselves in shackles when trying to collect God's tithes. Everyone seemed restrained just because Moullah's mother-in-law had gone mad.

The Israelites found shackles to be a happy medium between poverty and the heavy weight of silver. Hence, it became known as the new medium of exchange to create happiness. The Israelite accent eventually saw shackle pronounced *shekel,* and it turned out to be less of a restraint than Moonie experienced because it did permit the people to progress and prosper.

As people grew in numbers and spread throughout the world, so did *shekels.* Many nations developed with their own mediums of exchange which, in turn, were valued against the *shekel* in the same fashion and manner as set out in the laws of God, originally handed down to Moses of Levi. During this growth period, the priests were forced to accept the *shekel* and its widespread use. Their acceptance seemed to have something to do with the fact that they too were prospering from the medium of exchange. Although they no longer received silver pieces for tithes, they discovered they could maintain the same lifestyle with *shekels.* So *shekels* eventually made them happy and hence, the priests told the people God was prepared to accept Moullah's existence.

In the meantime, the two business partners lived well. Whenever they wanted to acquire something, they printed more *shekels.* Moullah was once again the wealthiest man in the world. But the more he had, the more he wanted – a strange aspect of human nature Moullah had heard of many years before in Egypt.

This strange behaviour caused people to be jealous of those who possessed more *shekels* than they – to kill for them – to compete – to seek revenge on those who pursued their *shekels* – and to steal from the wealthy. The very medium of exchange which made people happy provided a measurement for the strange behaviour that made them unhappy. For many of the victims of strange behaviour, *shekels* were evil and hence, *moullah* became known to many as the root of all evil. For those who prospered, notwithstanding the ethics of the day, *moullah* became known as the root of all happiness.

2

Biblical *Barter* – Part II

Moses Moullah died during the Year 1 B.C. Barticus died at the end of the first year of Christ, having negotiated a longer life. The relative timing of the two deaths was appealing to the priests because it afforded them the pleasure of witnessing Moses turn over his wealth to Barticus while on his death bed. The priests tried to impose the first succession duty on Barticus but failed to outwit the old master at the bargaining table. But when he finally died, Barticus had no heirs so all his wealth, plus that which was left to him by Moses, was vested in the church. It appeared that the priests had won in the end!

But had they? Moullah and Barticus had printed so many *shekels,* and the world had become so greedy and corrupt that far more *moullah* was required to purchase goods and services than when Moullah first shackled his mother-in-law. Because everyone wanted more and more *shekels,* they charged more for their goods and services. The world of business had overdosed on *shekels* and the population, being morally bankrupt from exercising man's personal traits, was happy for the most part.

So although God eventually got Moullah's wealth by making man mortal, it was worth considerably less than his priests had originally thought. Money had also become the symbol of immorality in society because it was usually the object of man's negative behaviour. The net result was that the priests, by their own vengeance for Moullah, now held a large amount of immorality themselves! Obviously, it was time for them to take a different approach, and revisit that which should be morally important to mankind – an appropriate beginning for *The New Testament.*

$ $ $ $ $ $ $

God dwelled for some time upon the different approaches He could take to reorganize mankind and to minimize immorality. Finally, He decided the greatest impact would be made by walking on earth through man. To have the right impact and be accepted by the masses, this mortal would have to be poor and humble but, at the same time, hold the power of God to teach a new way for mankind – that of love.

God sent this mortal in the name of His son, Jesus Christ. When He was born, three wise men from the East brought gifts to celebrate the birth of the Messiah. At the time, the three wise men did not realize their simple act of giving gifts would have the greatest economic, psychological and emotional impact upon man for centuries to come. The birth of Jesus was always to be celebrated by the giving of gifts. Gifts of the future would be purchased, and money would be required to effect those purchases. Many people around the world would profit by selling such gifts each year and other people would be employed by vendors, thereby enabling them to feed and clothe their families – hence, bringing comfort and happiness. Those who received gifts from this economic activity would also experience joy and happiness – rooted in the use of money!

Jesus grew up both in Egypt, and the small town of Nazareth in Judea. He was a carpenter for a short period of time but was generally unhappy with the *moullah* it paid.

Now Jesus had come to trust a friend, Plutomania, who offered to help Him become a teacher. Plutomania found in his subject natural qualities such as gentleness, kindness and care for people. He thought that, with these qualities, Jesus could teach by example. And, that teaching by example would be a natural way to gain power and control over wealthy people.

It began to work when Jesus became pious and travelled throughout Galilee teaching by parables while healing the sick. He developed a growing, loyal following of people who, in turn, brought gifts of *shekels* to show their appreciation and love – *shekels* which would have otherwise gone to the corrupt priests. This upset the high priests of the day and they felt threatened. The gifts of *shekels* were, of course, held and managed by Plutomania – who certainly did not feel threatened.

Jesus multiplies the loaves and fishes *as if they were* moullah

Jesus was in such demand He could not see to all God's teachings Himself, and so He and Plutomania decided to recruit assistants to whom the Lord's work could be delegated. Over time, it came to pass that twelve assistants were recruited and they became strong believers in Jesus and His power. They were His disciples and taught for Jesus in places where He could not.

Jesus used the power of God to heal and feed the poor. Once, He fed five thousand men with five loaves of bread and two fish. He continued to reach into a basket and remove bread and fish until all the people were content and full. The food multiplied as if it were *moullah*. Plutomania was moved by this and many times thereafter referred to his growing number of *shekels* as *loaves and fishes*.

Now Plutomania thought about his loaves and fishes and why it should be restricted only to Galilee. Why could *shekels* or *moullah* not be multiplied in other countries through the teachings of Jesus? He did not discuss this concept with Jesus but rather only sought permission from Him to travel the land delivering the will of the Lord.

And so he did travel, first to Egypt where he spread the word of God, then to Syria and Sudan. In all three places he developed a large following for Jesus, and his own loaves and fishes multiplied through gifts from the people. To assist people in giving gifts he helped set up a system of promissory notes in each of the three countries he visited. Because of his fondness for the quantity of loaves and fishes, he gave the new currency an appropriate name to reflect the weight and sheer quantity required to feed five thousand men. With Jesus, each pound of food fed one thousand men. And so, the *moullah* in Syria, Sudan and Egypt would henceforth be called *Pounds*. Centuries later, disciples of Plutomania imported the *Pound* into Lebanon, Malta, Cyprus, Ireland and the United Kingdom!

After many months had passed, Plutomania returned to Galilee and to Jesus. He told Jesus of his travels and work and Jesus seemed pleased. However, Jesus spoke of his concern for money or its generic name of *moullah* and the evil it often created. He felt in His heart that God wanted Him to somehow solve this problem. Jesus had concluded that those who gathered riches for themselves would not necessarily be rich in God's sight.

His disciple Paul felt very strongly about the evils of money and thought often of its problems. To Paul, there were many unruly, deceptive and vain talkers created by money or *moullah*. He felt this class of people would stop at nothing to acquire more *moullah,* and *shekels* acquired by such means were *filthy lucre* in the eyes of Paul – because of their dubious origins.

Paul also developed concerns about Plutomania's sincerity for Jesus' work, because of the great quantity of wealth he controlled and the extent it exceeded the meagre needs of the followers of Jesus. He began to feel that wealth was the underlying motivation of Plutomania instead of the teachings of right and wrong. Jesus did not appear to notice Plutomania's financial success but, to Paul, *Plutomania* was in an out-of-control state, and ruled by wealth. Paul referred to such a state as *plutocracy.*

Jesus, instead, was more moved by people who gave everything they owned than He was by Plutomania's accumulation of everything the people had given. This was noticed particularly by His disciples when a poor widow walked several miles to give an eighth of a *shekel* – which was all she possessed. Because it was everything, Jesus said she had given more than all the wealth accumulated from His teachings by Plutomania. Her contribution had the greatest might of all. And so from that day forward money with substance and meaning was known as *Widow's Mite*. Money or *moullah* used efficiently and carefully was *Widow's Mite* because it travelled further, acquired more food and purchased greater quantities of goods than foolish money.

Paul would write often of these matters and concerns to his assistant, Timothy. And Timothy was influenced greatly by Paul's cautions against those who preached against the Church and the true teachings of Jesus Christ. To him, those who did so would be swollen with pride and know nothing of life. They would have "an unhealthy desire to argue and quarrel about words, and this brings on jealousy, disputes, insults, and evil suspicions, and constant arguments from people whose minds do not function and who no longer have the truth."[21] To Paul and Timothy, people thought religion was a way to become rich, even though their characteristics were originally created by God – characteristics which drove men to conduct evil for profit or personal gain.

> "Well, religion does make a person very rich, if he is satisfied with what he has. What did we bring into the world? Nothing! What can we take out of the world? Nothing! So then, if we have food and clothes, that should be enough for us. But those who want to get rich fall into temptation and are caught in the trap of many foolish and harmful desires, which pull them down to ruin and destruction. For the love of money is a source of all kinds of evil."[22]

But Timothy neglected to reflect upon the characteristics of such people which he and Paul had discussed. He neglected to see that evil and wickedness existed long before wealth had been founded or created. So how could the love of money, riches or wealth be the root of all evil, especially when evil was created first?

$ $ $ $ $ $ $

With all this concern about the evil of *shekels,* Plutomania became insecure and frightened for the safety of his wealth. One day he asked Jesus if he could travel to Jordan to spread the Gospel. Jesus sent him, with His blessing, and Plutomania was glad he was permitted to leave Galilee. However, he did not know that he would never see Jesus or Galilee again.

Plutomania traveled on foot for many weeks before reaching Jordan. He began his teachings of Jesus but found it more difficult

---

[21] I Timothy, Chapter 6, Verses 3–6
[22] I Timothy, Chapter 6, Verses 6–10

to be accepted there than he had in other countries. The *moullah* did not flow as it had in Syria and Sudan. To improve his economic performance he developed an organization of Jordanians to become disciples. They formed a Jordanian school for teaching and printed promissory notes to purchase goods and services from other Jordanians who, in turn, donated a portion back to Plutomania. But Plutomania had to spend or shell out all his wealth to organize this Jordanian project. For two years he found himself shelling out *shekels* continuously to meet the expenses of the new currency required to pay for teachings of Christ. Since this was such an unusual problem when creating currency, Plutomania named the Jordanian money "shelling" which subsequently was pronounced *shilling*.

Just when the *shilling* was beginning to circulate properly and Plutomania was seeing a return on his investment, he was assassinated by one of his own organizers. Jealous and envious of Plutomania's control over Jordanian wealth, a Persian named Dinas stabbed him in the back to assume control over the financial empire.

Dinas expanded the operation into Persia, Kuwait, Libya and Tunisia. In these countries, he was overcome by his own vanity and hence, named the units of currency after himself. *Dinars* eventually grew in acceptance and became widely held in those countries.

Meanwhile, in Galilee, Jesus had become such a spiritual power that virtually all tithes and temple taxes to the priests had been re-routed to Him. The priests were jealous of this power and persuaded King Herod that Jesus was an evil threat to his power over the land.

Herod told the priests to find an informant within the group of disciples and bribe him for information. Since the disciples were not given *shekels* either by Jesus or Plutomania, they were ripe for a bribe. The priests studied the disciples carefully for they could not approach those who would be so loyal to Jesus that they would be betrayed. And so, they singled out Judas Iscariat as one who might *worship the golden calf.*

They met secretly with Judas and he agreed to hand Jesus over to them, at the first opportunity, in exchange for thirty *shekels.* He arranged for three guards to be waiting for Jesus right after supper. And when Jesus was arrested and taken to the High Priest, all the disciples ran away in fear. There, before the High Priest, a number of people bore false witness against Him in the absence of Jesus committing any real violation of the law. Based upon these accusations the priests sentenced him to death and crucified him.

When Judas heard of this he was filled with remorse. He returned the thirty *shekels* to the High Priest who refused to take the money back. Judas threw down the money but the Chief Priest said:

"This is *blood money*, and it is against our Law to put it in the temple treasury."[23]

However, being basically corrupt, they wanted to find a legal reason to keep the money. So they decided to take the thirty *shekels,* but only to buy Potter's Field as a cemetery for foreigners.

$ $ $ $ $ $ $

After the death of Jesus, the disciples continued to spread the good news about Him throughout Jerusalem, in all Judea, Samaria and to the ends of the earth. The Christian movement in Jerusalem expanded into other parts of Palestine and the Mediterranean world as far as Rome. Wherever the disciples of Jesus went, the disciples of Plutomania were not far behind. They developed and maintained close contact with one another even though one group was based in Jordan and one in Jerusalem.

One of Jesus' disciples, Paul, made a number of journeys throughout the world to spread the Gospel. When he passed through Cyprus he had to exchange some of his *shekels* for *pounds* which the hoarders of wealth referred to as *loaves* and *fishes*. Paul did not understand this until he realized Plutomania had been there many years earlier and had profited as he did in Galilee. Nonetheless, Paul became the first Christian to experience an international money exchange. Neither he nor the Cypriots knew how to value one *currency* against another so they simply agreed the two were equal and exchanged them at face value.

When Paul reached Athens, he found the economy was not as well developed as that to which he was accustomed. There, he met a disciple of Plutomania, named Drachmas. Drachmas had been assigned Greece, by Jordanian headquarters, as the next country in which to develop a strong local currency. After meeting, he and Paul ate supper together in a tavern to discuss the teachings of Jesus and the modern art of creating new economies.

Drachmas had been engaged by the Greek authorities to reorganize the troubled Greek currency. From Paul's point of view

---

[23] Matthew, Chapter 27, Verse 6

The disciple Paul founded international money exchange as he traded shekels *for* pounds *in Cyprus*

this was a concern, but he did realize there was no point to building a strong Christian movement upon a weak economic foundation. No gains would be made and so, it was agreed that Drachmas would complete his work first, before Paul began to teach Christianity.

Drachmas helped the Greeks mint a new currency in the form of coins and then organized the Greek people to exchange old worthless coins for the new *drachma* coins, as the authorities called them. And since Drachmas was to solve the problem of the worthless coins, he had to address the relevant value of the new coins. After all, why would a new coin, moulded by the same country, be worth any more than the old? The old coins were minted by the Greek authorities whenever they needed money – which was all the time. After years of such minting there were so many coins in circulation they were no longer pursued for value by anyone. And anything in such abundance and not the subject of financial pursuit became worthless. Drachmas concluded that over-running or inflating the population with coins would almost certainly lead to their worthlessness, and he did not want his name associated with such an outcome. Hence, history has credited Drachmas with the founding of inflation.

The Greek authorities were aware of his reputation and agreed to Drachmas' plan, which included:

- exchanging one new *drachma* coin for one thousand of the old Greek coins;
- no mass minting of the new *drachma* coin would ever take place; and,
- only ten per cent of the total population of *drachma* coins would be hoarded by the authorities.

According to Drachmas' thinking, these controls would hold the value of the currency and help the country develop an economy which would be much stronger than the rest of the civilized world – which was still printing currency to satisfy all its needs.

With that foundation laid, Paul began teaching the Gospel and convincing people that the false idols in Athens were not the true God. They were to melt down false gods, sell the gold and silver for the new *drachma* and donate the proceeds to the Christian movement. One by one, the owners of the idols were converted and they melted down their *sacred calves* and sold the residue for the new *drachma*. This whole process created tremendous pressure on the new *drachma* currency. It was in such demand by the former idol owners that its value increased dramatically. It required more and more melted gold and silver to acquire one *drachma*. Within five years, eighty per cent of the *drachma* in circulation were in the hands of fifteen per cent of the population – the former idol owners! The major portion of the country's gold and silver was now in the hands of the mass population while the *drachma* were in the hands of a few. Those few, in turn, donated money to Paul's cause. It was a primitive method of redistributing wealth but, nevertheless, it was effective.

Paul then travelled to Egypt where he found a group of wealthy businessmen who exchanged *pounds* for the *drachma* hearing of the great value associated with the latter. It would not be until after Paul left for Jerusalem that the wealthy Egyptian busi-nessmen realized that virtually the entire Greek currency was in their hands and hence, they had no market in which to trade their *drachma*.

Greece, on the other hand, was back to exchanging gold and silver, which was all it now had. There was no need to buy back its old currency given the renewed acceptance of gold and silver.

Drachmas demonstrated early principles of economic inflation and deflation for the physical well-being of everyone but himself

Meanwhile, in the absence of a market for *drachma*, the businessmen, and Egypt itself, were in danger of economic collapse. But the businessmen had heard of a clever economist bearing the same name as the Greek currency and who worked miracles for the Greek economy. They swallowed their pride and sent for Drachmas.

$ $ $ $ $ $ $

Now Drachmas had already concluded that he was in the business of reorganizing economies and currencies, not the creation of them. He found this far more lucrative as long as he was careful which currency he accepted as payment for his services. And the one lesson he had learned was to never again assign his name to any of the reorganized economies. This, unfortunately, did not prevent Greece from continuing with his name on their currency.

For the next fifty years Drachmas travelled from country to country in parts of Africa and the Middle East, teaching the economic horrors of printing too much currency. He became the only biblical authority on inflation – an unkind term assigned to him by the Palestinians because of his tremendous physical size. He suffered from an eating disorder and consumed more food than some countries did currency. He was purported to weigh the equivalent of four hundred and ninety pounds for most of his productive years. However, at the age of ninety-three he had become tired of being associated with inflation. And so, on his ninety-third birthday he stopped eating and five years later died of anorexia. Dying of anorexia was a fitting death for Drachmas. After all, he had devoted some fifty years of his career to the deflation of various economies throughout the known civilized world. Why shouldn't he have devoted his last five years to his own deflation?

Some time after Drachmas' death, Paul made another journey – to Rome. The sea voyage was treacherous and all aboard were scared. At one rough point, a young man came to Paul seeking consolation and he gave the young man comfort from the Lord. He asked the young man's name and Lirabus told him, vowing that if he survived the storm, he would become a Christian.

Paul said, "So it shall be." And not a hair on their heads was harmed as a result of the five day storm, although all the contents of the ship were lost.

Lirabus was true to his word. He converted to Christianity and followed Paul to Rome. He learned of Drachmas and the life and times of Plutomania. He never tired of the stories Paul told him during their long nights of travel. They made him dream; dream of wealth for himself, and the power he could have over people. Although Paul liked Lirabus, he found him preoccupied with the same thought which eventually consumed Plutomania, *moullah* – "galloping consumption".[24] In any case, the two were separated in Rome and Paul never saw Lirabus again.

Many years later, though, Paul came across a new currency during his travels. He had met two Romans who supped with him one evening and they insisted on paying for Paul's supper with their *Lira*. Paul enquired after the origin of their money. But the two Romans knew nothing of its origin except that it had been created by a man years beforehand who was driven to Christianity through fear during a storm at sea. They thought the man in question had moved to Turkey to organize a similar currency. Paul smiled quietly without explanation to the Romans.

---

[24] The 737 Papers, Chapter 4, Page 35

3

Basic *Bread*

Throughout the times of the great Roman emperors, Caesar and Augustus, money became a basic commodity among all households. It was generally understood to be the most reliable measurement for classes of people to determine their ability to subsist.

The *lira* was exchanged freely for grain, wheat and other staples. It was also accepted at inns, taverns and in the marketplace as a reasonable substitute for precious metals. But because the *lira* had penetrated society to such an extent, there were great differences between the lives of the rich and the poor.

In Rome, during Caesar's day, only a few thousand people were considered wealthy. And they, generally, included only those from the governing classes, owners of slaves, financiers and the like. This generation discovered that in a growing economy, the wealthy would go a step beyond that which Moullah had taken many years before. Instead of worrying about creating faith in currency by supporting it with camels or golden calves, the people of this time began to borrow *lira* on the strength of its own value. And, when called to do so, they would repay the debt with additional currency – no messy camels or extensive melting necessary.

As borrowing became prevalent, Rome generated huge debts and artificial fortunes – in what seemed to be a day. Contrary to the time required to build the city, frenzied finance was created a lot faster.

For example, many of the provincial governing positions were not fee-paying, but the governors were granted several residences in which to live, thus enabling them to borrow large sums of money. The residences gave them an appearance of wealth, and hence, initially making credit an asset – until they took advantage of it; then it became a liability.

Governors, however, had unique characteristics; they would neglect to repay these debts when they became due. Animosity grew rampant between debtor and creditor, but when too much pressure was placed upon a governor to repay he would simply pass a law eliminating that debt. This, of course, would outrage those who had lent the money in good faith. And, the whole system was aggravated somewhat by the existence of a law making it compulsory to grant credit to governors; to refuse loans to a governor was punishable by death. It seemed a trifle debtor-oriented for such an early society.

One such governor was Governor General Light (200 – 99) who was always somewhat light on cash. However, he possessed a house in the city of Rome, several villas in the country and a number of slaves. From 230 to 260, he accumulated debts of 5,000 *lira* just to feed, clothe and house his harem. He lived quite lavishly in light of his light cash position – assuming an endless supply of funds from his creditors. He drank a lot, attended all Saturday Christians vs. Lions games and became a terrible womanizer. After the games, he would come home drunk only to delight himself by abusing and scaring his harem at every opportunity – he was a real "harem-scarem".

Now, pressure was mounting on the Government of Rome during 265 to control Governor General Light. So the Emperor sent the city's financial expert to examine the financial position of Governor General. Deficitus Expendus examined Governor General Light's records, which he concluded were in an outrageous state, and pronounced the man valueless. He reported to the Emperor the phenomenon of borrowing money to fund current consumption of goods and services. The report upset the Emperor, and Deficitus was engaged immediately to conduct a imperial commission on governor borrowings and to make recommendations thereon.

Deficitus Expendus found that all governors throughout the country were abusing their positions in the same manner as was Governor General Light – and this was placing a great strain upon the country's economy generally, and the lenders specifically.

Emperor Augustus sentences all governors to public service – and creates the first civil service

Emperor Augustus was outraged at the findings of the Deficitus Expendus report. The finding that government personnel, at senior levels, were borrowing to eat and play was termed deficit expending or *deficit spending* after the author of the Imperial Commission.

Now the Emperor was obviously in a precarious position. He couldn't sentence all his senior officials to death for their indigent behaviour and fiscality for borrowed funds – because there would be no one left to run the country. Instead, he was forced to sentence them all as permanent servants of the country and they were to attend civil courses to improve their fiscal responsibility. The debts of the civil servants were paid by the country, their houses were taken from them and they were given a small annual stipend upon which to live.

It goes without saying that this was quite a culture shock and social adjustment for the governors. They were unhappy and concluded they should engage the Moabites or the Ammonites who were noted for their skills in organizing collective groups or unions – especially during the construction of the pyramids. And so they hired Alotless, the great-grandson of Lot, to help plead on behalf of the civil servants. Upon reviewing the objective of the civil servants, which was to improve their lot in life, Alotless advised he did not have the proper skills for the assignment. The civil servants would need the services of his brother – Alotmore.

$ $ $ $ $ $ $

The wealthy non-government class during the period of Caesar and Augustus had all the same luxuries, and more. The ultimate extravagance in luxury was spending great fortunes on imported treasures, baths, various types of entertainment, precious stones and, of course, elaborate food.

The most wealthy of men were said not to have been idle while enjoying such luxury. Many had a keen intellectual interest in literature, poetry and art. But, generally, they were only interested in that which immediately surrounded them. The problems of the people far away didn't seem to interest them whatsoever.

At the time, there were many private companies empowered by the Emperor to collect taxes and to earn a return for doing so. Those who managed such companies were private businessmen and certainly among the wealthy class.

One of the more renowned members of the wealthy class was Horace Bilker (301 – 89). He was the most notorious Bilker on his father's side of the family. And his tax company, The Bilking Company, was the most aggressive and, hence, the most feared company collecting taxes for the Emperor. But, by the same token, old Horace was the most successful *bilker* because he raised and raked in more *lira* in taxes than anyone else in the business.

Now, just as The Bilking Company was successful at wringing money from the public, it was also quite successful at dribbling it away – especially when it came to satisfying its owners.

Horace loved the finer things in life and was known to send for dancers, in far away lands, to entertain him and his friends. And since he was a bachelor and consistently in pursuit of the opposite sex, faraway propositions were expensive. He was never without at least six veiled ladies for whom he bought lavish gifts of lace and perfume.

Bilker was seen at all the fashionable parties in Italy – definitely a symbol of the elite and the upper class. He was considered somewhat of a rogue because of the dubious source of his wealth, and the immoral lifestyle which he lead. Nevertheless, among the elite he was viewed as a loveable rogue – at least as long as he lavished upon them all the symbols of wealth.

Horace took frequent vacations, surrounded by his entourage. Once, while holidaying in Northern Italy with twenty others, for all of whom he was paying the fare, he ordered a great banquet. There were dancers from Persia, lamb from Egypt and lobsters from Spain. The total cost of the feast, orgy and entertainment was 735 *lira*! But alas, Horace was in possession of only 625 *lira*. He was now in disgrace. Outraged at the thought, he sent a servant back to Rome for more *lira*. Four days later the servant returned with no money, so the owner of the inn, where they were staying, demanded an investigation by the Emperor and the death of Horace Bilker.

When the Emperor investigated The Bilking Company, he found it to be without any funds at all. Horace had pilfered all the assets to pay for his expensive lifestyle. Horace Bilker had not only *bilked* The Bilking Company, he had *bilked* himself, and there was no greater form of disgrace, at the time, than to be a self-bilker.

The Emperor divested Horace of his company, publicly ridiculed him and sentenced him to debtors' prison for life. He died a valueless and worthless man. But Horace's demise later resulted in some good. The Emperor eventually passed laws ensuring proper capitalization of tax companies, and created a tax regulatory body to ensure that fair trade practices were followed.

$ $ $ $ $ $ $

During the third century, the Roman Empire split permanently into empires of the East and West. But only the Eastern Empire survived the fifth century A.D. The capital was Constantinople. Such a chain of events did not matter much to someone like Impecunious (453–528) who could not even spell it. Well, he could spell "it", but he couldn't spell Constantinople.

Impecunious was a member of the poor, or lower, class. He was always short of money, and his employment possibilities were reduced with new trade laws previously implemented by an Emperor some years before. Since the great debt problems with the wealthy and the governors, all merchants were compelled to assume certain financial burdens. And because of such financial burdens, they could not afford to hire labourers such as Impecunious. People spent fewer *lira*, which had the compound effect of lessening demand for goods and services – the result being that by the fourth century the country was in an economic decline or a depression. The supply of precious metal had decreased and the currency had been debased many times. The people hoarded old currency and distrusted new currency to the point where economic confidence was lost in the governments of the day, and money ceased to be widely accepted. Finally, the economy collapsed.

Obviously, this state of affairs did not augur well for Impecunious' financial outlook. However, during 489 A.D., Impecunious' fortunes, or lack thereof, changed when he met a would-be princess in the marketplace. The would-be princess was Solidia Foundatious, heiress to her father's fortune. And to Impecunious' delight, she was attracted to him. They fell in love, resulting in a marriage that became as solid as a foundation. Solidia eventually inherited the family fortune, and Impecunious was never *impecunious* again. Money had brought him happiness!

$ $ $ $ $ $ $

During the late fourth century, a number of barbarian nations crossed the Rhine-Danube frontier and terrorized Western Europe, driving out the Romans. They were all Teutons but were composed of many different barbaric peoples. All these people, except for the Huns, established a permanent self-government in various parts of what became Europe. Most were tired of the nomadic way of life, with no place to call home. So, to over-compensate, they decided to pursue agriculture, and it didn't matter who had to die as long as the Teutons mastered their new vocation.

The Teutons took what they wanted from the local people. Although they were not savages, they were close to it – that is, they were coarse and rough. They were drunk most of the time and loved to gamble. And, when they crossed the Danube, they brought terror and horror, along with their lifestyle, to the civilized world.

The Teutons were ignorant and lazy too – which caused them to yield poor crops. So they frequently stole better crops from those who were more productive. They knew nothing about money because they either killed their food or took someone else's. They tried to barter with the Romans for hides, furs, wine, ornaments, food and slaves. But they didn't really understand value or how to assess it in a civilized fashion. So their houses were generally constructed of wood and mud, and the men preferred to hunt and fight rather than work.

Now, with all this whooping-it-up by the Teutons and their lack of respect for other cultures, the Romans tried to re-create a decent society and develop penalties for such unsavoury barbaric behaviour.

Since the Teutons had no sense of crime against the State, society chose to punish them for their offences through a system of fines. The fines usually went to the injured parties or their relatives who were prevented from seeking revenge against the Teutons. Fines varied, depending upon the damage to one's body or one's property. For example, if a man knocked out a neighbour's front teeth he would be levied a fine which would be twice as much as if he had knocked out his molars. If a big toe was cut off, the offender would pay the equivalent of several *lira* – a little toe would cost only a third of the fine for the big toe. The fine for killing a man was judgmental, but to kill a free man generally cost more than a slave. Money given to those injured, or to families of those killed, was meant to compensate for any loss or damage – kind of an early form of regulatory insurance through retribution.

The theory, though, seemed to contradict certain value principles established thus far in society. For example, one symbol of wealth was the number of slaves one owned. So presumably a slave was something of value to possess. But, if this was the case, why would one have received less in fines for a slave who had been murdered? Was there depreciation on slaves or was there an imbalance in economic justice?

And, if a man were to receive several *lira* for having his big toe cut off, he was limited to the total fines he could receive at the higher rate because of having only two big toes. This was an injustice, surpassed only by the fact that he could receive only a third of the big-toe fine for each severed little one. Therefore, using an example of 50 *lira* for a big-toe attack, a person could receive a maximum of only 100 *lira*. A fine for a little toe, in this case, would be approximately 17 *lira,* so, with eight smaller toes, the maximum fine one could receive from all severed small toes was 136 *lira*. If all toes were severed, the total take would be 236 *lira* – not a very big take for the pain involved. It simply wasn't profitable to engage in sufficient aggravation with a Teuton to have him remove all one's toes in exchange for a meagre 236 *lira* – which the Teuton had probably stolen from another victim anyway. At these ridiculous rates he may as well have taken the person's sole along with

Early retribution

his toes. Nevertheless, one could only conclude that such little compensation, by way of a fine, was only meant to stand in the shoes of the lost toes – it was not meant to create happiness.

While all civilization, morality and, eventually, economic wealth was declining in the old Western Roman Empire, the Eastern Roman Empire flourished with commerce, trade, light manufacturing and a stable civilization. Life was comfortable in Constantinople. There was no evidence of an economic decline there, nor were there any limiting fines related to toe-cutting. In fact, no one was ever known to have his toes cut off in the Eastern Roman Empire – it just didn't pay!

Now, somewhere around 800, there lived one of the more outrageous Teutons, Fastidious (Buck) Dibs. He was given his nickname "Buck" because of his teeth, but the man who first nicknamed him could no longer boast of the same physical feature. The man, however, did receive a fine.

Sometime around 811, Buck strayed into the Eastern Roman Empire, to Constantinople, where he found many opportunities to effect plunder, pillage and deceit. He thought he had died and gone to heaven. First though, old Fastidious decided to "survey the land". He was not stupid and therefore knew he had to understand the culture, laws and way of life of this strange land if he were to take advantage of it.

So he and his band of men stayed in a small inn toward the western part of the Eastern city. They drank themselves into a drunken stupor every night, and gambled with the local citizens – all the time trying to gain knowledge of the location of fortunes, the number of guards in each area, and the best time to pursue certain pilferage. For espionage purposes, they brought sufficient *lira* with them to honestly pay for their basic needs until they developed a dishonest plan to procure additional funds for future needs.

Fastidious Dibs was completing his verbal reconnaissance over the local traders when he came across a fun-loving scoundrel named Mammon. Fastidious and Mammon discovered, after several casks of wine, that they were both devoted to acquiring money in the same manner. This was just what Buck was looking for, a man made in his own image who was well-connected in Constantinople! A joint venture was bubbling and almost certainly imminent.

Mammon knew the location of all nobility, their guards, when shifts changed and when their houses were most vulnerable. So, after much planning, the two scoundrels elected to pilfer the money and jewelry belonging to Ab Norble. Norble was a backward person, notwithstanding his nobility, reflected by his desire to hide himself from his true identity – the Emperor's son.

One night when Ab Norble was out attending a remedial camel trading class, Buck Dibs snuck up on the guard and rendered him unconscious. Mammon went on ahead in search of money. Some time later, they located the *loot* behind a loose stone in the community bath – this was after turning over numerous stones. For an efficient escape, Buck took off, running fast with the money – with Mammon trailing behind. But, much to Mammon's surprise, the guard had regained consciousness, tripping him as he ran by.

A struggle ensued, resulting in Mammon being overpowered and turned over to the authorities for punishment. His friends ridiculed him for getting caught once again, as apparently he had a history of such luck. The legal authorities were used to seeing Mammon and, in fact, had convicted him of theft on several previous occasions – so much so that the judges actually termed the unsuccessful devotion to the pursuit of money as *mammonism*. Therefore, to them, Mammon had *mammonished* and consequently must be convicted of *mammonism*.

The penalty this time was death, but they rather liked the old rogue, so such a penalty seemed a bit harsh. They decided to commute the sentence if Mammon agreed to leave the country. This he agreed to willingly because he was still chasing Fastidious Dibs for his share of the *loot*.

Meanwhile, Buck Dibs travelled at an unbelievable speed to get out of the city and back to the now defunct Western Empire. His men were now calling him Fast Buck because of the speed of his daring midnight raid for money and fast exit from Constantinople. It was a logical nickname because they all knew the city authorities wanted first dibs on Buck, so time was of the essence.

Buck finally stopped to rest in a village which would eventually become part of France. But, seventeen days later, Mammon found Buck in the small village and demanded his share of the *booty*. Buck refused and a fight broke out during which Buck cut off all Mammon's toes. The barbarian authorities seized what was left of Buck's money and paid a fine to Mammon – that being the law in the Western Empire. Coincidentally, the total fine approximated half the total *booty* Mammon was entitled to, so equality was achieved in the end. And although Mammon had to pay a price to acquire his share of the money, at least it hadn't cost him an arm and a leg!

$ $ $ $ $ $ $

In the Western Empire, which became Europe, the barbarians wreaked havoc for many years. It was an atmosphere that forced a need for order among the Teutons. The Teutons took for themselves tracts of land from the inhabitants and then rented the property back to the natives in exchange for money. This made them somewhat happy and provided a feeling of security. But for the inhabitants, who now had to rent their own land, the money to be paid for the rent made them unhappy. This reverse economy was the beginning of the feudal system which became popular among tyrants all through Europe. Individual sections of land, seized to be leased back to their inhabitants, were called fiefs. And those who held the land were lords, while those who now had to rent their own property were called vassals.

The lords became very wealthy landowners as they gathered more and more property and, hence, rent. They became somewhat independent of the local governments as their fiefdoms were self-sufficient units. The vassals, also known as serfs, raised crops, made semi-processed food such as bread, and sold the produce at market in order to raise enough money to pay their rent to the lord. Money in France was called the *Franc* after the invasion of the Franks, and the use of it among the many fiefdoms created mini-economies within the country.

The vassals obviously had to sell enough wheat, corn and bread not only to pay the rent but also to generate sufficient funds to purchase life's other necessities. The rent was usually generated from the sale of bread the wives baked – and since the proceeds of the bread sales were the minimum amount of money required to retain and maintain the land, this money became known as *basic bread*. It came to be money required to purchase all necessities of life, and to maintain a subsistent and meagre existence – that is food, clothing and shelter for one's family.

Now *basic bread* for certain middle classes was a term which understated the true situation. The people were often heavy eaters who consumed multiple courses of food over several hours – presumably partly out of boredom and partly for public safety. After all, if these barbarians were eating, they weren't killing or maiming. *Basic bread* for such extremists consisted of bear, boar and deer along with vegetables and jellies.

Free men did not have to include in their *basic bread* the marriage fine, head-tax, and tallage at will – all common laws at the time. They were also free from heriot and castleguard and were permitted to come and go where they wanted. They farmed, raised chickens and pigs, and sold eggs and basic bread. But everything the free man did on the lord's land was measured by him in terms of money and was set out in a specific commercial contract between the two men.

The *basic bread* required for the poor was really basic. They lived in small, two room houses, constructed from branches, trees and mud. The roofs were thatched and the floor was dirt. One room was for grain, one for fodder. The homes were heated by a meagre fire in the centre of the room where peat or fagots burned in makeshift chimneys. There was usually a shovel, a pot and a ladle beside the fire oven, and there was one big bed for the whole family not far away.

Diet for the poor was basic bread, milk, oatmeal, cheese and vegetables. Meat and fish were rare treats.

All clothes were homemade from rough cloth and animal skins. The standard of living was very low, and only one crop failure had to occur to eliminate their *basic bread* and cause famine. A feudal war had the same effect because the object of a war was to destroy the other lord's crops. During the eleventh century, more than one in every four years resulted in famine – created either by war or crop failure.

So, *basic bread* required to pay for the lifestyle of the wealthy or noble class was a much greater quantity of money than that required for the vassals, serfs or the independent poor. The breakeven point for necessities was greater for the well-to-do – leading one to the conclusion that *basic bread* was not basic enough to be assigned a fixed value. Rather, it had to be considered a situational matter and, hence, a floating value from man to man.

The church itself had also feudalized during this process. Bishops and abbots held land from which they extracted the rents for their dioceses and monasteries. They, like the priests before Christ, leaned toward corruption and frequently used the rent monies for their own use or for political interests. This was of great significance in the interest of power because, by 1100, the church was estimated to own nearly one-third to one-half of the land in Western Europe.

The Barbarians, though, became more civilized with the feudal system and the influence of the church. They could now turn their attention to a more organized, orderly and systematic approach to semi-slavery, profiting at the expense of the people and various abusive economic schemes. It was time to turn away from the maiming and killing – although they still liked to drink and gamble to excess.

The various feudal wars, and those among the Teutons, saw the Western Empire become Europe by splitting into three kingdoms – that of the West Franks which became France – that of the East Franks which became Germany – and Italy.

All this created a big business for the church from landlording and agriculture. It had to collect all feudal payments from the vassals and make disbursements to the feudal overlords – or area managers. The bishops and abbots even considered the military business by maintaining their own feudal armies – a sort of collection agency to handle delinquent payers.

With the church once again attempting to compete with man for money and gain, it felt an overwhelming need to control every aspect of society – a flaw already depicted in *Biblical Barter, Part I* and *Biblical Barter, Part II*. The church just couldn't seem to see the difficulty in having its spiritual cake purchased with man's money, only to be eaten by fat, corrupt friars.

These flaws began to develop during the thirteen hundreds, or the last century of the feudal age. The mediaeval church, recognizing the fiscal problem, began teaching an ideal – termed "just price". It concluded it to be sinful to buy an article at one price and sell it at a higher one. To do so would be to take advantage of the buyer in the eyes of the church.

According to the church, the "just price" was to be determined by the cost of the raw material, in addition to the cost of the labour required to make it. The theory was based upon the belief that a man was entitled to earn a fair living in return for honest work, and a buyer was entitled to a fair or just price for the article. Buying an article and then selling it for a profit was not considered honest – perhaps a conclusion which could be applied to many modern day transactions.

Now the irony of all this was that the government and the church, while teaching the evils of profit, levied fines against those who made profits. Both the government and the church profited greatly from the fines without manufacturing a single article to be sold at all. They were making illegal profit by penalizing those making illegal profits! Moreover, when the church collected its feudal payments with its feudal collection army, and paid the overlords, it kept a share of the rent. The church itself was a middle man!

The church also prohibited the lending of money for interest – a transaction which was termed "usury" during the Middle Ages. Businessmen circumvented this rule by lending money at no interest, but putting penalties into the contract for late payments due on different dates. The problem was, though, that trade expanded rapidly during the twelfth and thirteenth centuries, and it could not continue to do so without interest payments and credit transactions. Voyages had to be financed, stores built, and raw materials purchased from afar and in advance. Churches also had to be built, and so the clergy found themselves borrowing money and paying interest, at such rates as twenty-five per cent, in order to operate. Toward the end of the thirteenth century, the kings were issuing permits to practice usury, but passed laws forbidding the lending of money at excessive rates – especially if the borrowed money was for the purpose of *basic bread*, or money used for necessities.

$ $ $ $ $ $ $

As trade grew and expanded, merchants required outposts in order to trade with other locations. These trading posts were the beginning of many small towns in England, France and Germany. They were usually built near castles or monasteries to protect the people from robbers and thieves. Within each town or city, weekly markets and fairs were held for the people to spend their *basic bread* acquiring meat, vegetables, clothes and odd luxuries such as fine tapestries, sculptures and the like. But mostly, the markets catered to the basic needs of all people located throughout Europe.

The towns, and trade alike, grew at a tremendous rate. As they became larger, the towns focused more on organizing the lives of their own people. It was not just the weekly market or the churches which brought the people together, it was the development of special interest groups. The merchants, craftsmen and labourers were beginning to polarize into separate spheres of interest and influence. No one group seemed to be happy if another prospered in any way more than they. A combination of the jealousy and greed, founded in *Biblical Barter, Part I* and *Biblical Barter, Part II,* was now quite well developed, so much so that these special interest groups would meet secretly to plan covert activities to destroy the progress of others. Tension among the groups was at a record level during 1100, creating an atmosphere requiring little effort to stir up the classes to a dangerous fever pitch. It took only one man.

That one man was Marmaduke Guilder (1069 – 1153), a descendant of the Moabites, who was raised in a small tribe in the northern part of western Europe. He was a union organizer like many of his ancestors, except that he never seemed to complete the organization of any one organization. Friends felt he had a learning disability which may have been hereditary. The effects of this disability revealed themselves through disorganization and the inability to complete any personal objectives. This feature of

Marmaduke Guilder preaches the benefits of a 'guild'

Marmaduke's character puzzled most who knew him, primarily because he chose administration as a profession.

Somewhere around 1110, Marmaduke Guilder wandered south into West Frank where he encountered the great tensions among the groups of merchants, tradesmen and craftsmen. He developed some affinity and empathy for the craftsmen and labourer groups – perhaps because his father had been a labourer. Nevertheless, he was a fire-and-brimstone speaker who possessed a marvelous ability to motivate violence in the hearts of men. His moving speeches encouraged the craftsmen and labourers to engage Guilder to organize them into an effective opposition to the merchants and businessmen. He was to be paid 1000 *Francs* if the results were successful. He began by taking the census of all craftsmen and labourers and obtained, from each, a written allegiance to him and his orders when it came to labour business against merchant business. There was no corner of any town where he did not speak while standing on a crate. In some cases, his speeches were almost to the point of yelling, and those who listened were afraid he was possessed by demons. He even frightened some of his own people.

Needless to say, the merchants felt threatened by this man Guilder. They referred to his organization as the "Guilder", later shortened to the "Guild". The Craftsmen and Labourers Guild terrorized the merchants and businessmen, hoping to coerce higher wages, while the latter tried to maintain the church's concept of a just price.

The threats the merchants received forced them to form their own guild in defence. They discussed the possibility of assassinating Marmaduke Guilder, but decided this would be a return to barbarism. One member suggested that, since the townsmen knew little about Marmaduke Guilder, they should dispatch one of their own men to Guilder's home town. This man was to sleuth out the origins of Mr. Guilder, looking for any information which might discredit him. All members of the merchants' guild agreed with this approach, and each contributed to the sleuth's travel expenses.

The sleuth was gone for eight weeks, and the merchants' guild had all but given up hope for his return. However, he did report back during the ninth week. He had located Guilder's home in the northern part of western Europe where Guilder's name was not considered reputable among the craftsmen and labourers.

Apparently, Guilder had created a currency, in that country, which bore his own name. The *guilder* was the product of a plan between Marmaduke Guilder and the business class. They had discovered the plan from certain biblical books and records concerning two people named Moses Moullah and Plutomania. The effect of the plan was to redistribute all the wealth from the masses into the hands of a select few. The working classes of Guilder's homeland, which later became Holland, considered Marmaduke Guilder to be the devil of the merchant and business class. But in West Frank, Guilder was posing as the champion of the craftsman and labourer!

The merchants were outraged and published the sleuth's journey chronicles in the newspapers the following week. Support for Guilder began to wane as his reputation was questioned. People began to feel he was a spy for the merchants and businessmen, and distrust in him grew quickly. As mad as he was, Guilder knew when it was time to leave – especially when he was being chased by one hundred people bearing wooden clubs. He caught one of his own native ships, just in time, bound for the flat edge of the earth. He was never seen again and, hence, was presumed to have fallen from more than just grace.

$ $ $ $ $ $ $

Fairs grew throughout Europe during the twelfth and thirteenth centuries as a source of entertainment to alleviate boredom from wars, famine and regular crime. The fairs usually had an array of minstrels, tumblers, dancers, jugglers and clowns, all of whom performed for money which might be available beyond the *basic bread* of those entertained.

The owner of one great fair which travelled Europe was Desbois (Des) Able (1183 – 1259). Des was an able Englishman from Middlesex. His mother was a Frank and his father was a Norseman – hence, the hint of both English and French in his name.

Des was educated in what is now Germany and so had a thorough knowledge of most of inhabited Europe at the time. He banded together the greatest number of acts into the largest European fair of the Middle Ages. He had the most famous jesters, tumblers, acrobats and dancers of the era, all of whom went about the cities and larger established towns, performing in tents set up for their temporary stay. Farmers, tradesmen and nobles alike came from far away to be entertained by Desbois Able's fair.

In France, it cost ten *francs* for each person to be admitted to the fair. Any food or candy purchased was extra, and there were certain charges for special performances. All this was very expensive for the average family whose members usually had to save money a year in advance to pay Desbois Able. It was money well in excess of their *basic bread,* and since the fair was the only entertainment which required money, the excess money saved was referred to as their Desbois Able money. This term, of course, became the subject of brutal changes in dialects, but it was most often pronounced desboisable or *disposable money* – meaning that money which was available to be disposed of.

Disposable money, although in different quantities depending upon one's station in life, meant the same to all people. And, to be frank, it only varied because each person's necessities varied. Necessities for Governor General Light were much greater than for Impecunious. The Governor's necessities included considerable entertaining and more than one house, while a substantial quantity of food was considered to be the only necessity for Impecunious – at least until he met Solidia, and then his necessity table expanded and required more *basic bread.*

Horace Bilker's necessities amounted to bilking more of everyone else's *basic bread* – and hence, their necessities became his necessities.

Fastidious Dibs didn't seem to consider money itself as a necessity, but rather the speed at which it could be acquired. And, to acquire it at the expense of Mammon was a luxury not a necessity.

Marmaduke Guilder thought the pursuit of strong unions, secure jobs and higher wages were his necessities for living, but not at the expense of the profit he had made in his currency operation.

So one man's concept of necessity was another's disposable money. And that which was disposable was not of necessity – only necessities were basic and, therefore, paid with *basic bread*.

4

Past *Pelf*

The old feudal system represented semi-slavery for the peasants. Contracts with their lords usually provided for free field labour as well as payment of rent for the use of their own land. This environment nurtured friction between the lords and serfs because the lord usually wanted his free labour at a time when the serfs could least spare it. And the serfs were a fair target for this free labour because they had perfected agriculture. So if they were ever to earn more than their *basic bread* from agriculture, they had to produce more than a subsistence level of crops – that is, more than their families could consume, hence, crops to earn disposable money. But the forced free labour component of the feudal economy prevented the serfs from producing more for themselves.

The growth of towns provided the market for any agricultural surpluses. The townspeople had greater disposable money, generally, because they were businessmen, nobles or people with steady healthy incomes. Now the serfs had the capacity to produce and sell agriculture in excess of their own needs, but the demands from the lords for free labour interfered with the serfs' ability to produce and sell in the town market places. Moreover, the work for the lords was basic and hateful, and consequently the serfs were not motivated to do it well. This, in turn, aggravated the lords since they also were not yielding the maximum crop to earn more money.

Some lords realized they could generate higher crop yields and money by hiring men for wages. Where this was done, the serfs were forced to pay additional money to lords in lieu of providing extra labour. But this had an interesting compound effect on the serfs who then had to produce and sell more product in order to pay for their increased necessities of life – that is, the rent. The peasants just couldn't seem to win or better their lot under this economic system. The lords, on the other hand, who received money in lieu of labour had such money to offset the payment of wages associated with the newly hired labour.

For those serfs who paid money in lieu of labour, their ties and obligations to the lords were reduced – and there was less day-to-day contact. To a greater extent, a serf was becoming physically freer, and the authority of the lords over them was being reduced to just a financial obligation.

The serf was now motivated to work a longer day, primarily for two reasons – he had more free time to devote to his own agriculture, and extra efforts were now for his own benefit, not for a lord. In addition, a serf had to earn more to pay the extra rent, but this did not seem to outweigh the benefits of his being master of his own turf. Anyone who succeeded and became his own landmaster was termed a serf 'n' turf.

Working from daylight to late evening a serf 'n' turf prospered beyond his wildest dreams. And with the extra or disposable money they earned, many serf 'n' turfs bought their freedom from their lords altogether. So, by the beginning of the 1400's, this quiet economic revolution eliminated virtually all the old fiefdoms.

The labourers who worked for the lords for wages were in short supply. This was so much so that many of the serf 'n' turfs began to work for their old lords voluntarily, for wages, during their spare time. This seemed to be a slight conflict of attitude when one considers the serfs' long fight for freedom. Nevertheless, it provided greater disposable money and enabled them to finance a growth far beyond their *basic bread*. The serf 'n' turfs now not only had greater freedom but also more money with which to enjoy it. Money had greatly enhanced their happiness.

Now, during this era the population suffered from the Black Death – a mysterious illness which lasted from 1348 – 50. In England it had its most profound affect, killing thousands of people without so much as a medical clue. And, unfortunately, the epidemic took a greater toll on peasants and labourers than on the monied class – perhaps relating to a better diet or lifestyle among the latter. In any case, the epidemic made the working class weaker, thereby rendering scarce the labour resources. The end result was a higher demand for the survivors and, hence, higher wages for their labour. For those who were not able to work, the lack of money was a constant source of aggravation. For those who could work, the extra work generated greater amounts of disposable income. The unable viewed the pursuit of money as an evil necessity which made life miserable. The able seemed to enjoy more happiness!

So it went…one man's happiness was another man's misery. And no one knew this more than the feudal lords. Now they had to pay higher wages for the performance of the same work – not because the work was more demanding, but because there were fewer workers! This was an absurd option to wealthy lords who objected to such economic reality through their merchants' guild which they evolved into a lobby group for government intervention against higher wages. Their power ultimately proved to be strong enough to convince Parliament to pass legislation fixing the level of wages.

This marked the first intervention by government into free enterprise and the forces of supply and demand. And it met with just as much success as any later government intervention. The working population was outraged at an attempt to limit its progress. It resulted in retaliation by the serf 'n' turfs who left the lords who abided by this new law to work for lords who did not. Anyone who supported the government's new law could not attract hired help to do their work. So, economically, the law self-destructed because those who lobbied for it in the first place were those who suffered the greatest loss of money by its very existence – the lords.

Even though neither the wealthy nor the poor were happy with the government legislation to restrict wages, the government continued to enforce the law for many years. But, since both the supplier (labourers) and the consumer (lords) wanted to supply and demand during this period, they were quite happy to work together to avoid the law. And so strangely enough, the law the lords lobbied for, against the labourers, seemed to bring the two closer together in the name of a common cause – more money. The lords were prepared to pay above the legal wage to motivate serf 'n' turfs to work harder which, in turn, generated more produce and, hence, money for the lords.

Now, for the first time in history, one saw two opposing groups equally satisfied with their position concerning money. They were brought together by a common enemy – government!

Yes, a body incorporated to prevent two sides from winning against each other encouraged them to become closer to pursue the common goal of money. Thus, one experienced another first – the beginning of hatred against oppression and government. The hatred of government brought unification to people which had, and continues to have, a positive affect upon the spirit of people. Who said the enemy of my enemy is my friend?

This all may sound insignificant, but one must remember that, to this point, man had either been against the Church or another man. There had not been a case where money helped unify man against an organization such as government. Money had brought happiness to two groups in an environment where one would surely be otherwise unhappy. Now there was a third party who could be unhappy – government. It became easy to hate those who wanted to govern and who opposed free will or the forces of money. It was not money that was the root of all evil. It was government!

$$\$ \, \$ \, \$ \, \$ \, \$ \, \$ \, \$$$

Between 1300 and 1500, France and Britain were at war.[25] The British held certain lands to which the French laid claim as their natural heritage, particularly the rich wine properties near the port of Bordeaux. The King of England collected a high tax on the wine exports from this country, and this tax was the envy of the French.

It is not the intention here to recount the events of this war. However, it holds significance in the history of money because it was economically draining for both countries. And the fighting had to be financed in some way – usually by the hard work of the common people and higher personal taxes.

The ultimate spirit and national feeling among the French eventually saw the English driven from the land. And it so happened that this *esprit de corps* raised substantial sums of money from the French peasants of Bordeaux who, in turn, were prepared to donate a certain portion of their disposable income to rid themselves of the English. But although the peasants gave freely and at will, the extra payment impeded their own financial progress. And this became particularly annoying to them since they had just paid their lords for freedom from serfdom.

The English financed a substantial portion of their side of the war by selling the Bordeaux wines back to the French elite. The latter could not do without their fine wines no matter who they had

---

[25] A World History from Ancient Times to 1760, Chapter XI, Page 402

to buy them from. There were just certain basics to be included in their *bread* or *moullah* budget. But the wealthy French were so discreet about their wine purchases that no one ever knew they had helped finance both sides of the three-hundred-year war! Their love of wine added to the English coffers, and their love for their country added taxes to the French coffers. If the French had not been so set in their dietary ways, this protracted war would probably have been retracted earlier.

The English elite, on the other hand, were not as highly taxed because the French bought vast quantities of their own wines from English governments, thereby substantially defraying the cost of the war. So, even though the English may have lost the Bordeaux country, the loss was not one which was felt financially on an individual level. In other words, the average Englishman didn't care about, nor did he have any interest in, retaking the Bordeaux. Once peace was struck with France, the English could actually buy the Bordeaux wines at a cheaper price than when they occupied the territory themselves. Apparently, French labour was much cheaper than English. And because the French were so laden with taxes to pay for the war, they were prepared to work for anyone at any wage – which turned out to be less than the labourers from England who made the wine during the war. When analysed, the French fought for three hundred years to earn less money managing the lands they were seeking to acquire. But they had successfully reacquired that land and, as a result, assured themselves of a lower standard of living from working the land.

On the other hand, it appeared the English found happiness because they didn't have to pay for their three-hundred-year war personally, and they subsequently could buy their same exquisite wines for less money. Everyone was happy!

$ $ $ $ $ $

While the effect of a macro-economic war was being felt by England and France, their people continued normal day-to-day living, at least as much as they could expect. The English were noted for their spirit just as much as were the French. However, the English seemed to be better able to cope emotionally and financially and, hence, were less likely to let world events interfere with proper tradition. They managed their money well by practising the principle of consistency; that is, they constantly spent and saved the same amounts of money, in the same proportions, throughout their lives. They were master-planners of frivolous detail, and anything which happened outside their plan for day-to-day life was very off-putting and, in all likelihood, would provoke bad form for several days.

An example of English planning for the time was demonstrated by Sir William Pin (1433 – 1503). Sir William was said to be so precise and finicky that he ironed his boot laces every day and refused to speak one day out of every fortnight. His clothes had to be prepared and laid out eight days in advance, and any disorder within his house was met with tremendous rage.

Sir William Pin owned and managed a town-planning company which was frequently consulted by the government on the appropriate manner in which to expand growing English towns. Sir William provided advice on efficiency, town-planning, locations for merchant areas, and water and sewer. He was constantly spending time improving his foresight which gave rise to his silence every fortnight.

At home, Sir William Pin drove his wife mad with his idiosyncrasies. He was so consumed with planning that he suffered from psychological disorders. This was first diagnosed by a London psychiatrist when it was learned that Sir William had gone as far as to allocate certain funds for his wife to purchase straight pins.

Straight pins were scarce during the fifteenth century and were reported to have been sold only twice a year. Therefore, a certain amount of planning was required if one's wife was to be satisfied with her quantity of straight pins. Sir William was exact in this area because he set aside a small allowance for his wife to purchase straight pins on a regular basis. She was considered to be a very lucky Pin to have pin money accumulating in a fund while her husband was being pronounced crazy.

Sir William drove his wife mad with his habits, only to be diagnosed mad himself. In 1495, he was placed in a state institution for the remainder of his life. The government, in turn, revoked his knighthood, and his wife, Lady Pin, inherited all the pin money as the sole beneficiary of the Pin Estate.

The people were taken with this unusual situation and thereafter referred to pin money as that which was bequeathed for small or frivolous items such as pins. But Sir William Pin's estate was not frivolous, by any standards. Consequently, Pin money, through

Sir William Pin fathoms the creation of a separate budget for his wife to buy straight pins

time, became *pin money* because of Sir William's name rather than because of the intended purpose of the money.

$$\$ \$ \$ \$ \$ \$ \$$$

The decline of the feudal system also brought a cautious mistrust of the church. Because so many of the lords were overlords for the church, the serf 'n' turfs, when they were just serfs, began to question the motivation of religion. And it was this growing mistrust of the church which resulted in a corresponding growth of power for governments in England and France. Even though no one trusted governments any more than the church, their growth became popular because it was fashionable or sporting to criticize, second-guess and even vote out of office different governments. This could never have been done with the church because it was so autocratic and assumed its role was to dictate to the people how they should live. It was clear that government, with its dual role to govern but yet seek support of the people in order to survive, was a new and strange phenomenon for people.

In the British Isles and France, political parties were formed to support candidates for elections and to raise money for those people to seek election to office. It was a game for some, a living for others. But for all, it was at least a spectator sport. For Harper Shielding (1430 – 1503), it was the only way of life.

Harper was born and raised in Kilkerry, Ireland, where he joined the political party of the business class at the age of eighteen. He campaigned vigorously for the party almost full-time, and because there was little or no pay for the job, he lived a subsistence life – only the basic of *basic bread* was available.

Harper Shielding was elected to Parliament at the age of twenty-eight. He was the youngest man ever to represent a segment of the Irish people, but as an "Irish chancer"[26], it came with ease.

Now Harper had a cause. He wanted the Irish people to have a currency which carried some weight. After all, the English currency was at least a *pound* so why should the Irish not have a currency which commanded similar or greater respect or weight in the world. Secondly, the Irish had had particular difficulty with their paper currency – it was constantly being devalued as inflation continued at a high rate.

Harper wanted to change this economic environment, and to do so, he conducted a considerable amount of research. He read the works of the biblical economist, Drachmas, who had had considerable experience with the same woes. Shielding was convinced that if Ireland were to return to a minted *coin* to replace its paper currency, known as the *light pound*, all money problems would be solved. The name *light pound* was not only an indication of its value as compared to the English *pound*, but also an historical link with Governor General Light – the ancient Roman Governor who over-borrowed, over-spent and over-drank. There is no historical evidence to explain why these characteristics were associated with the Irish, but nevertheless, that was what Harper Shielding had to face.

He made many speeches throughout Ireland for the coin cause. Finally, in 1481, a Bill was introduced in Parliament creating a new coin in the name of its champion, Harp Shielding – or the *harp shilling*, as it was pronounced. The name *shilling* came from the ancient Jordanian money which was created by Plutomania and which coincidentally resembled Harp's last name. After the coin's issue, it took almost ten years to take all the *light pounds* out of circulation. Harp was placed in charge of the project and decided to offer one *harp shilling* for every ten *light pounds*. This seemed logical to him from an economics point of view; however, he didn't

---

[26] The 737 Papers, Chapter 5, Page 49

take into account any possible non-numeric reaction from the people.

People had striven for and achieved freedom to accumulate small quantities of money throughout the feudal era. This was the only satisfier for any insecurity. Now, a politician elected to Parliament at twenty-eight years of age was going to request ten units of currency from each of them and replace them with one! Even though the coin was heavier and, hence, carried more weight than the English *pound*, the ratio of ten to one was difficult for the people to accept. Accordingly, a long struggle ensued for Harper Shielding. And because there was a struggle between Harper and the people for the acceptance of the coin, it had an image problem. Everyone jeered at the coin, causing its intrinsic value to be somewhat less than that intended by either Parliament or Shielding. And the fact that the coin had an imprint of a harp actually served to cement the public's dislike for it.

Nonetheless, Harper finally won the exchange war and received a commendation from Parliament for doing so. The *harp shilling* had made Harp Shielding happy – finally! As for the people, they found the image problem of the coin made it less acceptable as a medium of exchange in Ireland – and even more so in England. In Ireland, it was supposed to equal twelve *pence* or basic units of currency, while in England, it fetched only nine *pence*. This was not much better than the original Irish *light pound*. So, because of its lesser value, the *harp shilling* soon came to connote cheapness – and hence, was not as much a source of happiness for the people as was originally intended. The unacceptability of the coin eventually caused Harper to be forced out of office in 1493.

Harper's son, because he bore the same name, was also forced to face humiliation and intense dislike from the people. Even though Harper Jr. was nicknamed Punt by his father, his birth name followed him everywhere. Life was intolerable for Punt, and consequently, he was determined to rectify the economic chaos his father's *coin* had caused – and to restore his own name to grace, although he did not want to be called Grace. The name Punt was bad enough.

So, in 1493, Harper Shielding ran against Harper Shielding for the same seat in Parliament. The only issues were currency and confusion among the people as to who each candidate was.

Harper Shielding debates coin versus pound *note with Harper (Punt) Shielding during the 1493 Irish elections*

Harper Shielding campaigned on his ability to repair the damage he had caused, while Harper (Punt) Shielding promised the issuance of a new *pound* note which would be easier to carry and more acceptable to both the public and international trade. The campaign was long and vicious, causing no end of delight to the public. Some people even worked for both sides just to maintain the fever pitch of the competition.

To add to it, the Shielding family, who were normally dyed in the wool Publicans, were split down the middle. Harper (Punt) Shielding forced the creation of a new party just to oppose his father in this election. And because Punt represented the rebirth of his father both physically and economically, it was only natural that his party become Re-publicans. So history saw the first split of a family along party lines – Publican and Republican. But when the votes were all in, Punt, the Republican, won by one vote. Harper was bitter and always suspicious that his wife had voted for her son instead of her husband. He always claimed that was just the sort of thing one could expect from her.

In any case, Punt and the Republican party made good their election promise and returned the country to a new *pound* currency, one that had a much greater public acceptance level. The *punt*, as the new *pound* was named, enhanced trading with England and restored honour to the Shielding name. Oddly enough, Harper Shielding enjoyed a certain amount of this restoration to honour too – presumably because he bore the same name as his son.

This whole process, of course, was a sort of "reverse vicious-ness"[27] or reprimanding of Harper Shielding. He attained happi-ness first by conquering the public with his *harp shilling*. But he subsequently lost his job to Harper (Punt) Shielding who in turn brought the *punt* into circulation, the reputation of which returned happiness to Harper for the second time. The currency seemed to be the medium, not only for exchange, but also for achieving an equilibrium for happiness between the Shieldings and the public.

$$\$ \, \$ \, \$ \, \$ \, \$ \, \$ \, \$$$

All the while Sir William Pin and the two Shieldings were living separate micro-economic lives, significant events were taking place on the macro level. The established European coun-tries were financing voyages to discover new lands – to lay claims in the name of their country, expanding the wealth of countries as well as men. Up to the Middle Ages such travel was dominated by the Italians and Moslems, but Spain, Portugal, England and France also began pursuing new routes to the East to enhance trade with China.

The European communities had their appetites whetted by Marco Polo's *Book of Various Experiences*.[28] His father and uncle, known as the Polo brothers, travelled on more than one occasion to China where they learned to make shirts and pyjamas. They became journeymen at the trade for two reasons. Firstly, they had to journey to learn the trade, and secondly, they had to attain a level of expertise sufficient to obtain their craftsmen's papers. And because the Polo brothers had to travel so far to acquire their trade, the lengths of the journeys were equated with the work required to master a trade – to accomplish a trade then meant that one became a journeyman.

Nevertheless, the Polos returned to Venice to open their own Polo shops. These merchant shops were successful enough to finance other journeys to new lands – particularly for the son, Marco. From their travels, navigation charts were prepared to

---

[27] The 737 Papers, Chapter 4, Page 33
[28] A World History from Ancient Times to 1760, Chapter XLIII, Page 437

describe the routes, lines and any distinguishing markers. The other European countries followed suit.

Portugal became interested in Africa and the setting up of trading stations there in strategic locations, one of which was the cape of "Good Hope". Christopher Columbus, Vasco daGama and John Cabot all made voyages westward trying to reach the East. All were independent mariners who spent as much time trying to finance their voyages as they did making them.

The kings of all the European countries were constantly being approached to finance such voyages. It was a big risk for them, but if the riches were there, the return on the investment could be handsome. For example, Vasco daGama returned to Lisbon in 1499 carrying a cargo which yielded a net gain of six thousand per cent on the money invested.[29] This was only one of many successful voyages which saw Western Europe develop significant new trade routes. The exchange of interest and financial efforts in favour of exploration saw the decline of Italian cities and the replacement of the Mediterranean by the Atlantic as the main route for growth of trade, empires and civilization.[30]

$ $ $ $ $ $ $

Once established, the trade routes were lucrative, but also dangerous. The vast amounts of gold, silver and treasures being returned to Spain, England and other parts of Europe were subject to the hazards of piracy. And although countries and their people were becoming more wealthy, they were losing a considerable amount to major piracy operations such as that of Captain John T. Boodle (1500 – 69), who made his home in the South Atlantic Islands – believed to be what is now the Caribbean.

Boodle searched out well-travelled trade routes by stealing maps and other navigational documents from ships he captured. Once the routes were known, Boodle would lie in wait to attack ships returning home to Europe laden with treasures. After he committed each piracy, Captain Boodle quickly returned into hiding on one of his islands.

John T. Boodle populated a number of what are now the Caribbean Islands with prisoners taken from the ships he plundered. With the treasure he seized, he financed the construction of entire communities on these Islands, including sugar, rum and fruit businesses. Labour was cheap since Boodle had a captive

---

[29] A World History from Ancient Times to 1760, Chapter XLII, Page 429
[30] A World History from Ancient Times to 1760, Chapter XLIII, Page 440

John T. Boodle sails into a Caribbean port after confiscating treasure from a Spanish galleon

work force. And he successfully used this resource to process and manufacture goods for resale in America and Europe – very much a self-financing empire, more efficient and profitable than the European treasure voyages.

John's treasure acquisitions, or *boodle* as his captives called it, began to annoy the Spanish during the early 1530's. And so they sent war ships out to sink all Boodle's ships. But by this time, John T. was a well-established highwayman of the seas and could not be caught. He commanded an intensely loyal crew, and since the captives were all given jobs in a warmer climate, they had no reason to plot against John T. So he lived out his days a wealthy man, having made crime pay. The Caribbean was built economically and populated entirely as a result of *boodle*. All were happy!

$ $ $ $ $ $

The *boodle* that made it safely through to Europe was reinvested in the Americas. Spain and England built splendid navies to escort biannual voyages seeking more *boodle* and land in the name of their countries.

In the case of Spain, the tremendous wealth acquired within a short period of time caused great difficulties. Its small population was now in possession of a great deal of money. And, as already established, whenever someone possessed a great deal of something it became worth less, resulting in rising prices which, in turn, created inflation once again.

Spain was not well developed in the manufacturing area and history saw it develop only agriculture to any great extent. The government tried to take on too much of the exploration pie, and without the manufacturing infrastructure, it could not sustain the economic pace. Hence, a lot of its wealth left the country in search of a better return on investment, while goods and services came to Spain searching for higher prices. All this economic strain on Spain caused it to fade from world power after the seventeenth century.[31] Portugal experienced similar economic failure.

The changes in world trade routes from the traditional to the more profitable created new trading centres. The major trading centres turned to interior Europe in general and Antwerp in particular. Venice was displaced as voyages were now nearly all around the Cape of Good Hope and not through the Mediterranean. The lack of trade through Spain and Portugal reduced those two European countries to poverty once again – no *moullah*, no happiness.

Now, an important observation has to be attended to. During the process of discovering new lands and treasures, the European economic units switched from cities, towns and guilds to the greater areas of different countries. The old trading system, which focused internally from community to community, was now dwarfed by exotic Eastern and Western world trade activity. The spirit and ambition of the people to acquire greater wealth broke down the guilds which had originally restricted international trade and the activities of merchants.

Commercial agencies were established throughout the known world to facilitate trade with individuals in "mother countries". Funds flowing back to The Netherlands, France and England were greater than that required by the recipients for their *basic bread*. This, in turn, forced the establishment of some system or place to lodge their money. Banking businesses commenced in major cities where the wealthy could make their disposable money lodgements.

The sixteenth century was also the time the wealthy first began to experiment with the concept of business partnerships.

---

[31] A World History from Ancient Times to 1760, Chapter XLIV, Page 444/5

Businessmen, of course, were driven by greed, and when they could not finance operations and voyages to satisfy their appetites, they joined together to finance different segments of each operation. Partnerships were formed to accomplish large business transactions and to spread the financial risk. The first joint stock company was actually formed in 1553 in England.[32] Capitalism was born!

The credit for the founding of capitalism was given largely to Woody Barker (1498 – 1576). Woody, at the age of twenty-five, began a lumbering operation in England. It was his belief that with all the world trade, *boodle* and travel, a building boom in England and the Americas was not far off. Unfortunately, at the time, Barker could not afford to fund the operation himself. But determination drove him to his two best friends to discuss a possible partnership or company to buy land, cut trees, log and saw the forest into building boards.

Woody Barker's friends were an unlikely combination. One was known as Francis the Torturer (1503 – 72) who made a healthy living as a contractor for the king in Liverpool, England. He was engaged to carry out hangings of criminals and an assortment of tortures on those who had difficulty conducting business with the king's men. Because no one wanted the contract, and the work was so ghastly, Francis maintained the job for some twenty-five years. He was feared by all, including the innocent, but as long as he was well paid he was not bothered by his own image. He received one hundred *pounds* for hanging a man, two hundred for a decapitation, three hundred for severing limbs and five hundred for using the screw in exchange for blood-curdling yells. Hanging paid the least because it was a relatively clean and easy task. Screwing, on the other hand, was time consuming as it would sometimes take a week of constantly raising the screw before clients talked. Although torture by screwing required more time, it was Francis the Torturer's specialty. And because of Francis' popularity in the area of screwing, he raised a lot of money by *raising one's screw*. As a result of his success, Francis had ample *disposable lucre* to become a partner for Woody Barker.

The second friend and potential partner was Jack Nimble (1504 – 79). Jack began his business career as a banker. He opened a bank in London in 1534 and almost immediately began minting a silver coin which traded for about nine *pence*. Nimble was able to sell a considerable number of these coins shortly after issuance,

---

[32] A World History from Ancient Times to 1760, Chapter XLIIV, Page 449

not because of their value but because of the unusual pliable nature
of the silver coin. It could be bent in and out of shape with relative
ease – a quality which gave the public a feeling that it lacked
strength. Consequently, its value never really grew beyond nine
pence, and the nimble *ninepence* traded as a token or collector's
item. Nevertheless, Jack Nimble made a fortune selling his *nimble
ninepence* during the first three years of its minting.

Woody, Francis and Jack agreed to meet, over a pint of meade,
at the Boaring Pig Pub in London on January 27, 1553. There they
discussed a possible partnership and how it would work. Finally,
after three days and seven kegs, the three shook hands as equal
partners in The Nimble Wood Joint Stock Company. Francis' name
was left out because he had passed out. Instead, the remaining two
gave honour to the pub, which was a joint, named after the owner's
stock in pigs.

Woody Barker said, "If we are going to be the first limited
partnership, we must have the operation properly capitalized. I
could not live if, after my death, the first joint stock company was
a failure."

Jack Nimble replied, "I don't really understand your logic, but
I'll concur anyway."

"If any one tries to put us out of business, I'll torture the bloke
for free," butted in Francis.

And each of the three partners contributed five thousand
pounds to the beginning of The Nimble Wood Joint Stock Company.

Woody Barker became the first president and immediately
bought land from the church in the south of England, near the most
active port cities. Francis was in charge of labour supply, generally
because of his persuasive talents. Jack was assigned the responsibility of finance as he was the banking and minting expert of the
three.

While Francis was organizing labour and the building of a
sawmill in the south of England, Jack and Woody went to the
Americas. They landed somewhere in what is now New England,
and after a frustrating search, they bought a thousand acres of
timberland to the north of where their ship landed.

"Now, I think our most efficient and effective approach, Jack,
would be to build a sawmill here, exactly the same as the one
Francis is building back home," observed Woody.

"Well, Woody, we ought to be very careful here. You know *money doesn't grow on these trees*," stated Nimble.

"Wrong!" exclaimed Woody. "If we cut down this timber, saw it into lumber and sell it to the builders, it will become money. So in effect, the trees will grow into money – just by cutting and stacking them, one can *make one's pile*."

"Okay, okay," begged Jack, "but we are over our expense budget already with the land and sawmill in England. So we have to be careful to save enough money not only to build the Americas' mill, but also to operate it once it is built."

"Well, let's see. Let's think for a moment and review the budget figures and the cash reserves we have left," said Woody pensively. "I think you may be right, Jack. It looks like we may not have the wherewithal to do it all. But wait a moment, Jack. You still have a whole chest of those useless *nimble ninepence*, don't you?"

"Yes, as a matter of fact, I do," replied Nimble," but I don't understand the significance of your point."

"Well, my good friend, the news of the worthlessness of the *nimble ninepence* has not yet reached the new world, has it?" queried Woody.

"No, it hasn't – at least I don't believe it has," pondered Jack.

"Okay, here is what we do," concluded Barker.

The next day, Jack Nimble began visiting all the settlers who were in need of work. He offered to pay them English or Irish currency in return for labour to cut timber and build The Sawmill of the Americas. Within a week, Jack had rounded up thirty men who would help build the mill. They worked very hard during the hot summer of 1554 in return for all the *nimble ninepence* Nimble had brought with him. When all was completed, The Nimble Wood Joint Stock Company owned the state-of-the-art sawmill which would normally have cost five thousand *pounds*. But the whole operation was constructed for about five hundred *pounds* worth of the *ninepence* tokens.

Jack said, "My God, we have increased our capital or equity by a net amount of approximately forty-five hundred *pounds*."

"That's right," smiled Woody, "and with the heat this summer and the amount of hours to build this beauty, I would say one would have to call it *sweat equity*. But no matter how you account for it, it is a windfall."

Francis the Torturer demonstrates the then modern labour negotiating techniques

The mill went into production during the spring of 1555, almost a year after the sawmill in England began its operations. With a year of operating experience in England, the company was finding it difficult to control its labour expense. Jack and Woody had received word that Francis was having some difficulty keeping labourers at the wage rate he was prepared to pay. Barker and Nimble thought Francis to be the best person to cope since he was current on all the modern reprimanding techniques.

For the first year of operation of The Sawmill of the Americas, most of the production was shipped back to Europe for resale. As the settlers possessed only tokens, there was no possibility of selling lumber locally for any early gain to the company.

By 1556, The Nimble Wood Joint Stock Company was selling about fifteen thousand *pounds* worth of lumber a year at a profit of about seven thousand *pounds*. It was, to say the least, doing well financially. All excess lodgements were made with the Bank of England where they were paid interest for its use by the bank.

At the second annual partners' meeting, the Corporate Chancellor of the Exchequer, Jack Nimble, reported that the reasons for the company's success were cheap labour, high lumber prices, and the avoidance of borrowed money. The company's sweat equity had provided what would have otherwise required bank borrowings. That was the reason for corporate success and, hence, must be the formula for future profits!

However, not long after the annual meeting, signs of labour unrest began in the Americas' mill. It appeared the labourers, the same men who had built the mill, felt they should have part ownership of the company. They had realized the *nimble ninepence* was worth only about a tenth of their labour value, and they had been *bilked*. As relations intensified, Barker sent for Francis the Torturer to mediate the dispute. Francis arrived during the summer of 1557, rearing for the challenge. A meeting of the labourers was called for early August and Francis acted as Chairman. He assembled a limb-screwing machine with which he normally presided over such meetings.

Francis began the meeting by introducing himself and offering a brief personal resumé as well as a demonstration of his limb-screwing machine. The men seemed somewhat taken aback by Francis' rules of order for a meeting but they were determined to stay and make their point.

Following the demonstration, Francis said, "Now, we hear in England that you blokes are not happy. Is that right?"

"That's right," replied a spokesman boldly.

"Who are you?" yelled Francis.

"Erasmus Pelf, sir."

"Well, Pelf, state your business here," bellowed Francis.

"It's like this, sir. The company had us build this mill and then paid us with token or cheap money."

"What's wrong with that?" retorted Francis.

"It just doesn't seem fair," replied Pelf, "that the company should do that and then expect us to work here for wages while you *make your pile*."

"*Make my pile!*" yelled Francis, "Did you or anyone else invest cash in this company?"

"No, sir."

"Did you or any of the other men have any *pounds* to invest in this company?"

"No, sir, we just have the *nimble ninepence* we were paid to build the mill and the *basic bread* you pay us to operate the mill."

"Just as I thought," sighed Francis with contempt. "Would

you be accumulating any *basic bread* or would your wives have any *pin money* if there was no mill?"

The men looked at one another and then the spokesmen said quietly "No."

"Well," said Francis, "each man has three choices. He can work quietly and be paid in *pounds*; he can quit; or he can test out my new limb-screwing machine. And, Erasmus Pelf, I can guarantee that if you choose option number three, you will be a past Pelf."

Pelf looked at the other men who, after a few moments, gave him a nod. He looked down at the ground and stated with authority, "We will all work quietly for *pounds*." But everyone could tell by the look in Erasmus Pelf's eyes this humiliating experience meant they had not heard the last of Pelf – he was not to be past Pelf.

Francis, on the other hand, feeling quite the triumphant labour specialist, was on the next boat for England.

$ $ $ $ $ $

While Woody Barker, Jack Nimble and Francis the Torturer were making their pile, the European business community was growing faster than the inhabitants really realized. The downfall of the old feudal system, together with the growth of capitalism, and the influx of *boodle* created an economic leap never before known to mankind.

England invested in and controlled many faraway lands – such as India, parts of the Middle East and the Caribbean, as well as most of the Northern Americas. France also held parts of North America and the Caribbean, while Spain still maintained a substantial portion of culture in the Southern Americas. All such major European countries had taken in far more wealth than they needed to sustain themselves. Hence, the growth and expansion of capitalism and the development of hundreds of limited partnerships or "joint stock" companies such as The Nimble Wood Joint Stock Company.

With all the sea travel, ship-building flourished, the insurance industry was born in Antwerp,[33] and people could afford to engage commissioned salesmen to go to market to buy and sell for them. This commercial explosion provided a ripple effect throughout the economies; those who had money spent for pleasure and those who did not have money received it for wages – all acquiring happiness from some amount of it.

---

[33] A World History from Ancient Times to 1760, Chapter XLIIV, Page 449

Antwerp also developed the first "exchange".[34] There was no evidence that shares or stocks in companies were widely traded, but there was substantial speculation on both commodities and money exchanged between countries. The new exchange, which was built in 1531, had engraved over the doorway, "For the use of merchants of all nations and tongues."[35] This was to symbolize a rapidly expanding trade that was free, on an international basis, and very much based upon the desires of the individual and not the state.

Manufacturing meant making things by hand. And even in these early days of capitalism, there were a few small manufacturing plants. With the economic explosion they became capitalized and the craftsmen, who normally worked for themselves selling their own goods, were incorporated into joint stock companies and paid wages.

Religion, although still an important influence upon the people, no longer controlled and dominated their lives. The Church had been so closely associated with the old feudal system which suppressed the progress of the people that its place in society was redefined as that of spiritual guidance only. It totally ignored the new wealthy class, was controlled by nobles, and consequently, no longer held the economic power to force the direction of the people.

Because of the Church's lack of understanding of the middle class, it lost most to the Protestant movement and reformation. The economic explosion and the tremendous increase in wealth seemed to bring happiness at the time to all except God's priests. This appeared to be a continuation of the evolution of man and God, experienced first by Moses Moullah and Barticus.

The Catholic Church also reformed during the late sixteenth century, but it was too late to attract the middle class back to the original church. The two religious groups clashed throughout Europe leading to many wars, the most brutal of which was the Thirty Year War (1618 – 48). This war resulted in a tremendous loss of life – wiping out entire communities and towns. There was an astounding destruction of culture, economic power and morals. Also, the conclusion of the war left smaller pockets of minority religious groups throughout various parts of Europe, a social problem which would cause friction between religions for centuries to come.

Money gave them the resource to fight, while moral and religious differences gave them a cause to fight. Both religions

---

[34] A World History from Ancient Times to 1760, Chapter XLIIV, Page 449
[35] A World History from Ancient Times to 1760, Chapter XLIIV, Page 451

claimed to follow God's teachings, and those of Jesus. But each was prepared to break God's law by killing for power. One is reminded of those first few days of history when God instilled those basic characteristics of:

- competition
- jealousy
- anger
- killing, and
- revenge

These characteristics, built into man's nature, had truly become the root of all evil. Money had become a resource, along with man's brainpower, to satisfy the human need for growth and power. Without any one of these resources, it appeared man would be destined for stagnation – a condition that, if not rectified, generally creates rot and odour. But what could be more rotten than killing one another in the name of the same God who teaches one not to kill?

$ $ $ $ $ $ $

During this economic growth period The Nimble Wood Joint Stock Company continued to prove that *money grew on trees* – cutting, logging and sawing its way to wealth. The employees in America made good their word to work quietly – at least for about five years. They were reasonably happy earning a good wage in *pounds* – all except Erasmus Pelf. His bitterness following his humiliation by Francis the Torturer festered and grew with each passing year.

In 1562 Pelf visited a friend in Jamestown, Virginia. The friend was an ex-banker who had been run out of Yorkshire, England, for an alleged misappropriation of funds. Erasmus explained the whole story of The Mill of the Americas and the cheap *nimble ninepence* the men had received for building it.

Pelf's friend said, "Well, why don't you mint your own *nimble ninepence* and beat the partners at their own game?"

"How do I do that?" queried Pelf.

"Well," said the friend, "first you get all the men to agree to a plan to exchange their *pounds* for a new *coin* – perhaps you call it the *pelf coin*. They will do this if they are convinced it is for the good of the nation and that they will profit by regaining their lost wages."

The pelf coin *minted from the* nimble ninepence

"As you know, the company's sales have now become dependent upon the settlers in the new world. The settlers have earned money now and are able to buy lumber from The Nimble Wood Joint Stock Company. The men who worked there have already bought lumber to build homes for their families with the *pounds* they received for wages."

"They will buy more lumber with the new *pelf coins* and we will see what we shall see."

So Erasmus Pelf followed his friend's advice and minted a shiny new silver *coin* by melting down all the *nimble ninepence* paid to the men for building the mill. It was a special coin not only because of the source of its raw material, but also because it was the first American coin. It was a handsome work of art, and it had to be if it was to be successful.

Because religion was so strong among the settlers, the *pelf coin* had "In God We Trust" minted on one side. This was to have the special psychological effect of appearing to be blessed by God. And, since the Pilgrims, Quakers and other settlers had read about Moses Moullah, Barticus and Plutomania during the long winter nights, it was significant to have God support the new currency.

Erasmus Pelf, on the other hand, thought it particularly ironic that God's battle, through the ancient priests, for control of money should be honoured by minting a coin with his trust.

The opposite side of the coin had a picture of the settlers clearing the land for the mill – again, a psychological effect of reminding the men they had built the mill for nothing.

These two psychological factors made the acceptance of the *pelf coin* surprisingly easy among the people. Also, the fact the coin was made from silver gave it a certain perceived intrinsic value.

Within eighteen months Erasmus Pelf had spread the acceptance of the coin within one hundred miles of the mill. Everyone was using them to purchase groceries, haircuts, shaves, whiskey at the saloon and furniture. The local banks were accepting them as deposits because the bank, in turn, could spend and invest the money. The Nimble Wood Joint Stock Company was somewhat leery at first about accepting *pelf* as payment for lumber. Their concerns dwindled, however, when the banks began accepting the coin.

By 1565, virtually all the sales of the mill were paid for in *pelf*. Then Erasmus began reversing his procedure. As the mill accepted more and more *pelf*, the merchants and suppliers of services accepted more and more *pounds* from the public. This was so effective that by January 1566, almost all the *pelf* was in the hands of The Nimble Wood Joint Stock Company, and all the community *pounds* were in the hands of the people. Then, on February 1, 1566, no one within one hundred miles of the mill would accept *pelf* as payment for wages, goods or services. The mill, in the absence of funds other than *pelf*, could no longer pay its debts. Hence, it became insolvent and collapsed, and had to be sold by its head office in England. Erasmus Pelf bought the mill at an auction and ran it successfully on the *pound* currency. The people were delighted that Erasmus Pelf had reversed the trick on Barker, Francis and Nimble – and he did so with the very same token *coinage* that the partners had used on him!

When Francis the Torturer found out about this trick he went into a rage which lasted for about a week. He tortured everyone in sight, making sure that no employees in the British mill got the same idea. He boarded the next boat for the Americas in search of Erasmus Pelf. And when he arrived in America, he chased Pelf for two years before he caught up with him. It was a vicious fight between the two before Erasmus died. Francis, wounded badly, stood over Pelf's body.

"I told you more than ten years ago that you would have no *pin money* for your wife, no *basic bread,* no *moullah*, unless The Nimble Wood Joint Stock Company paid you to work. I gave you three choices and you chose the first which was to work quietly. Well, I also told you that option number three would result in your passing. In the end, that was your choice – now you and your coins are both *past pelf.*"

5

Reign of *Ransom*

With the rapid development of capitalism putting pressure upon English society and its economy in every direction, the individual's life was, nevertheless, quite a "pleasurable rut."[36] The country, beaming with prosperity and contentment, was an apt reflection of the prosperity of its people. High society developed and distinguished itself from middle and lower classes through the study and discussion of literature and poetry, attending plays and the ballet. Ownership of art was an excellent way to express one's snobbery and to provide a certain amount of "one-upmanship" during discussions about town. The characteristic gifts from God of competition and jealousy were running rampant.

The middle classes were the old guild members who had prospered through the great *boodle* era to effectively springboard themselves into respectability in their own eyes. They could now pay for their basics, plus enjoy a number of luxury extras without much financial strain.

If there was an upper and middle class, there had to be, by definition of logic, a lower class. The streets of London were still populated by beggars, thieves and prostitutes. The middle class had more sympathy for them than did the upper class because they were there once themselves. So they would periodically toss the down-and-out a *harp shilling* or a *nimble ninepence* to be of assistance. Actually, it was somewhat ironic because the down-and-out currencies of all Europe usually ended up in the hands of the down-and-out. Now, this is not to be misunderstood – the poor, although still poor, were much better off during the new capital era than

---

[36] The 737 Papers, Chapter 7, Page 66

under the old feudal system. During the feudal era, such people were not tossed anything, except out! This is why one considered the new capital economic explosion good for everyone, albeit by different degrees.

Even at the beginning of the new capital era there existed in England for many years The Knights of the Round Table. They were appointed by the King to be special consultants in the area of monarch protection and national defence. They usually consisted of a small number of very brave and honourable men who were chosen to meet frequently at a huge round table with the King. The most famous of the Knights was Lancelot – a handsome and very intelligent Knight from Kent. He was a descendant of the biblical family of Lot, and was frequently called upon to joust – hence, his name.

Now Lancelot's heritage may explain his excessive sympathy for the lower class – an opinion which he was not afraid to express around the King's court. The expression of such opinions was not considered socially acceptable for the time and so he was frequently admonished by the King.

Because there was a lower class, there was a tremendous growth in crime, and the creation of the famous "highwayman" style of robbing, which Lancelot took an oath to eliminate. The highwaymen terrorized every road in and out of cities and towns. And they would hold their catch at sword point, strip them of all their *boodle*, and then disappear into the forest. The money was *boodle* to the people because John T. Boodle used the same technique against European ships on the high seas.

One of these highwaymen was the legendary Robin Hood who, by Lancelot's own account, was impossible to catch – although the King was somewhat suspect of the sincerity of Lancelot's attempts. And there was no question that Lancelot would have been beheaded had the King known that he not only knew Robin Hood, but that they were friends!

Now as the legend goes, this man Robin Hood led a band of jolly thieves who achieved total happiness by stealing money – the absence of which would have left them without "self-actualization"[37] and Lancelot without employment. God appears again! Man is not supposed to steal money, but if he does, others will be paid money to stop him.

---

[37] The 737 Papers, Chapter 12, Page 129

In any case, Lancelot was convinced that Robin Hood was different. He had been persuaded by Hood's men that all funds seized during robberies were given to the poor – a chord which struck the strings of the harp, on each of the fifty *harp shillings* Lancelot received monthly for risking his life.

To Lancelot, Robin Hood's army was dedicated to creating a socialist society; that is, redistributing the wealth from the upper to the lower class or, in other words, robbing the rich to give to the poor. As Lancelot's ancestors were a long line of union and guild labourers all the way back to the construction of the pyramids, he felt Hood's heart was in the right place and his approach logical.

The two men used to meet secretly in Sherwood Forest to feast, laugh and drink meade. Lancelot was always given Hood's next robbery plans so he could be somewhere else when it took place. This procedure was a necessary caution as Lancelot not only had to worry about the King, but also the Sheriff of Nottingham who had a vicious dislike for both he and Robin. The arrangement between Lancelot and Robin Hood went on for many years as both *made their pile* trying to outfox the crown's men.

The King at the time was Richard the Lionheart. He was a fierce, tough, yet fair, fighter and ruler. Lancelot was intensely loyal to him, as was Robin Hood in his own way. Hood would have been the first to go to war to defend England and her honour, not to mention her steady flow of *pin money* he snatched from passersby.

Richard's brother, John, was very eager to become King, but since Richard was young and in reasonably good health, John's succession in the near future was unlikely to happen. This prognosis was intolerable to the not-so-clever John. But he did have clever friends in the King's court, however, who banded together to plan the kidnapping of the King, thereby giving way to John usurping the throne.

John's friends thought of paying bandits to commit the evil act and set out to find the most competent of the time. A fatal mistake was made here as there was an effective communication network among the bandits of Sherwood Forest. Because there was honour among thieves, John's supporters could not talk to anyone in Sherwood without Robin Hood hearing of it.

So the loyal Robin Hood met one night with Lancelot to discuss the matter and the appropriate strategy. Ultimately, they decided to wait until Richard was actually kidnapped and then to meet with the bandits. When this had actually happened and John thought himself safely on the throne, there was a meeting of the bandits, Robin Hood and Lancelot. From that meeting, Lancelot learned that all other thieves in the forest had tremendous respect and loyalty for Robin Hood – it was all for one and one for all!

Now the bandits were paid only one hundred *harp shillings* to commit the kidnapping crime. Richard, who was held hostage by the bandits at the meeting with Lancelot and Robin, thought he was worth more than that. Angered by the matter, he told all they would be pardoned if they would restore him to the throne and rid him of any further threats.

Robin had a plan. The bandits must now demand a *ransom* or sum of money from John or they would expose the new King for what he had done. So a note was sent to John to this effect – demanding a ten thousand *pound ransom*. This was the largest ransom ever requested in history – *a King's ransom*. The note also said that if the money was not received within forty-eight hours, they would free Richard and expose the whole affair. An alternative was also proposed. If the bandits received twenty thousand *pounds*, they would kill Richard, and John's problem would be permanently solved.

John, needless to say, was in a panic. He could not take twenty thousand *pounds* from England's treasury without The Chancellor of the Exchequer authorizing it – and the latter was loyal to Richard. John could only raise this money himself by borrowing beyond his capacity to do so – but to be exposed as his brother's kidnapper was fatal. So he borrowed the twenty thousand *pounds* and selected the bandits' proposed second alternative. He followed the instruction on the ransom note carefully and delivered the money to the designated location.

Robin's men picked up the money and delivered it to the bandits, Richard and Lancelot. When Richard learned that John had to borrow the money to pay the ransom, he told the bandits they could keep it and they would still be pardoned for their loyalty to him. They banded together behind Richard and marched on London. And when John saw them march on the castle, led by Richard, he fled. When his creditors found he could not repay the loan, they petitioned him into debtors' prison to which he was finally sentenced to life.

Richard made good his promise to Robin Hood and the bandits. He pardoned and permitted them to keep the *King's ransom*, a phrase which would refer to large amounts of money for all times. Who said crime didn't pay? As for Lancelot, since all bandits were now pardoned, he really had no work or responsibility. His job was terminated, permitting him to be with those with whom he had sympathized most – the lower class.

$ $ $ $ $ $ $

Needless to say, the kidnapping of Richard the Lionheart made all kings somewhat nervous. All were trying to anticipate who might be plotting against them next, and how they could protect themselves. A *King's ransom* made them a target for every highwayman or thief in their respective countries. Throughout the 1600's, 1700's and 1800's, many successful kidnappings took place where *King's ransoms* were paid and never recovered. Throughout this period, capitalism, manufacturing, banking, communications and travel all advanced – as did the quantity of money in circulation. Hence, this era, although preoccupied with industry, was really the *reign of ransom* in the eyes of all European kings.

$ $ $ $ $ $ $

Throughout the three hundred years of the *reign of ransom*, the kings of the world focused more on their own safety and less on the affairs of state, parliament and day-to-day country problems. This period provided parliaments with a narrow window in history, when they could expand their power, take complete control of tithes and taxes, pass countrywide laws, and generally insert themselves between the king and the people. With this, of course, came a growing expectation on the part of the people for better government, responsible action and no interference with commercial activity of the business class.

The feudal system had left such an negative impression upon the merchants and craftsmen that its effects would not be forgotten for many centuries. The French were the first to recognize this through the doctrine of laissez-faire, and it was supported by Adam Smith, the Scottish Economist, in his work *The Wealth of Nations* which appeared in 1776.[38]

So at this stage in the mediaeval and modern history of money, events have taken place which have changed the use of money and the lives of people who were affected by it. It is time, then, to make a brief review of these events in order to solidify one's understanding of their effect upon the future.

---

[38] The Concise Encyclopedia of World History, Chapter 15, Page 35

First and foremost, the feudal system created an individual thirst for money and economic freedom that lords, churches or governments were never able to quench. People would only trust themselves to direct their own business affairs.

Secondly, because the church controlled almost two thirds of European land during the feudal era, God, through his priests, was not only the first landlord but the largest. Never again would the people permit the church to control both such vast wealth and their souls.

With this history, it was only natural to expect people not to permit government the opportunity to become a new lord over their land. So business, commerce and industry forced growth at a tremendous rate during the middle and more modern ages, free from government control.

There were other significant events. After all, any nation in an *impecunious* state would not all-of-a-sudden have the wherewithal to develop a sophisticated capital economy. No. There were forces other than the rise of individualism and the decline of church power – the primary one being the vast amounts of *boodle* returned to Europe from the colonies, in such a short period of time. This provided the otherwise missing ingredient to create capitalism in a world of *basic bread* – that is, capital itself.

Everyday life began to focus on how to acquire more capital. Better ships had to be built to handle ever-increasing cargoes; navigational tools were forced to be upgraded and seamen taught; construction of residences and commercial buildings increased to accommodate the influx of people and the growing trade. And this, in turn, placed tremendous pressure on craftsmen to build, manufacture and deliver more goods and services at a faster rate. But the craftsmen could not keep pace. Each was restricted by his own personal capacity – and, to be self-restricted was almost certainly uncomfortable. Technology had come a long way but not far enough to cope with the demand for disposable income and the people who wanted to part with it.

All this quickened the business pace to such an extent that communications were forced to improve. People wanted more knowledge about world affairs and its effect on *moullah* – also at a much faster rate. Newspapers improved in quality, speed of delivery and accuracy. "News-ships" shuttled back and forth between the Americas and the Far East at regular intervals. It was all this business information and revitalized communication which helped Woody Barker, Jack Nimble and Francis the Torturer *make their pile* and prove that money does grow on trees.

Now one comes to an interesting human phenomenon in history that was implied but not stated in the list of traits given to man by God, and documented in *Biblical Barter, Part I*. Flowing naturally from the traits of negotiating and reneging on agreements was that of laziness, the desire to acquire more and more for oneself while, at the same time, working less and less. One could say this whole concept approaches the greed factor as well.

In any case, Pheneous Midas (1701 – 98) made a study of this trait in an attempt to understand Europe's rapid economic change and, perhaps, to offer some solution for its tremendous demand for goods and services, a demand which was increasing consumer prices.

Pheneous Midas discovered from the written works of history's scribes certain developments concerning these human traits. Man first substituted animals for human labour. Then sentries were replaced with watchdogs, oxen were used to plough fields, and donkeys were harnessed to haul goods. This division of labour between man and animal raised the value of animals, making them subject to purchase and sale as well as to theft. Money values were assigned to different animals. And in many cases, the animals sold for more than slaves, mainly because they cost less to feed, were more loyal and didn't escape from time to time.

Midas also studied the use of water power which man harnessed along with windmills to operate rudimentary equipment. Animals, slaves, water and wind were all used separately and for different tasks, but each had its own limits – which were far surpassed during the *reign of ransom*. By 1742, the world could not develop any further economically without some form of reliable, tireless and powerful resource to help meet the growing demand created by *boodle*. Since the problem was easily isolated by the ability to deliver goods and services, the issue in Pheneous Midas' mind was clearly one of productivity. How could England and the other countries produce more with the existing resources they controlled?

He approached the appropriate authorities in parliament who were trying to cope with such economic crisis management. He proposed they hire him to study the problem of productivity and report back his findings and suggested solutions within three years. After a month of deliberation they agreed to Midas' proposal and granted him an annual stipend of five hundred *pounds.*

Armed with his historical research he began examining the whole concept of division of labour. Up to now, each craftsman completed all the manufacturing of his product from start to finish. He bought his own raw materials, designed his own products, then built or manufactured them to personally sell in the marketplace. A good craftsman who took pride in his work could make only a few items a week, as time would permit only such a small quantity when he was performing all functions alone.

Midas thought, what if he performed only one function repeatedly – such as buying or selling a product? What if the craftsman completed one function continuously to the exclusion of all others? He might become more efficient if he repeated the same function than if he continuously switched functions. That, Pheneous Midas thought, would greatly improve man's output as a resource. And if a number of men could be placed in each function, the output of a finished product would be that much greater – a compound increase in productivity would result!

Midas tested this theory with sword manufacturers. By persuading four craftsmen, who would otherwise compete with one another, to join together as a joint stock company, Midas succeeded in having one craftsman negotiate the purchase of steel, one operate the hearth, one hammer the sword into shape, and one market the product to knights, noblemen and the like. The test results showed that the four craftsmen could complete and sell ten swords per week using division of labour, as opposed to four swords per week separately. And they weren't competing with each other; they were working toward a common cause. All benefited from the profit of the six extra swords manufactured and sold. That was it, thought Midas. To date, man's division of labour had only been between wind, water, animal and man himself. It had never gone the next step of dividing tasks in a logical manner, among men themselves. So Midas' study clearly supported a new concept which he termed the "production line."

The production line conclusion was all well and good, but in the example of the sword craftsmen, the market demanded twenty when they could make only ten together, or four separately. It was clear that Midas was only half way in terms of solving the supply and demand problem. But he had pushed man as far as he thought he could, and during his experiments, man was showing signs of boredom with doing the same task all day, every day. Pheneous thought the creation of some sort of tool or apparatus that did not tire or become bored, and which completed a task at a much faster rate than man, was the possible answer.

Pheneous thought of man's experience with wind and water, but in their basic state these sources of energy weren't considered consistent or reliable. What if man could contain them someway in order to maintain an even or constant resource flow? Pressure of some sort would almost certainly be required, as well as storage of a special nature, to safely contain any such pressure.

Midas explored all sorts of makeshift tanks for and from windmills, and he even visited Holland to consult the Dutch on their expertise but came home with nothing but a pair of wooden shoes and a bouquet of tulips for his wife. He went into his house and plumped himself down in a chair by the fire. His wife was preparing their evening meal of boiled potatoes, roast beef and pudding. All was on the stove and smelled good, but Midas was tired and depressed with his lack of progress. So he did not pay normal attention to the household culinary production line. His wife left the room for something and was gone for some five or ten minutes during which Pheneous heard a whistling sound; it intensified with each moment. When it reached a fever pitch, he looked into the matter only to find the lid on the pudding pot was too tight and the boiling water had no ventilation. As he approached the stove, the lid blew off nicking his forehead. What force, he thought. He stopped – and pondered for some time.

"That's it!" he exclaimed.

"If I could harness boiling water on a much larger scale, I could use the pressure from the steam to force movement of some sort on a regular and uninterrupted basis. It would be .. a .. a 'Pudding Engine'."

Immediately he began to draw, and within a week had prepared blue prints for the Pudding Engine. It was a large five hundred gallon tank, air tight, except for a hand-release for man in case something went wrong. At the front was a large door to a fire box. After all, Pheneous was, in substance, designing one large stove to boil one large pudding pot.

Pheneous Midas' first pudding engine

He persuaded his four sword craftsmen to build the pudding engine for him. But when finished, it didn't do anything except make steam. So Pheneous said to his four helpers, "What is the most mundane task that you do during your work?"

"Help you!" shouted one.

"No, no," said Pheneous. "While making swords?"

"That would be the hammering of steel," said another. "The smith work is definitely the hardest, the most time-consuming and repetitive task."

"Can you make me a hammer in somewhat the shape of the human hand with an arm slightly longer than a human one?" asked Pheneous.

The four thought for a moment, stroking their beards. "Yes," they said in unison, "we think it can be done, but the smith work will have to be done by hand."

"Good," smiled Pheneous. "If you do it right, it may be the last smith work you do by hand."

And they did do it right. It took, however, another week for them to make an attachment to connect the arm to a wheel and to mount the wheel on the Pudding Engine, near the vent cap – so it would turn under pressure from the steam. It worked! And the more water and fire the more steam, then the faster the wheel would turn, resulting in more frequent hammering by the artificial arm.

It worked by feeding the steel on a continuous basis through one side of the arm. And after five weeks of trials, the Pudding Engine plus the division of labour among the four men raised the output of swords to an average of twenty-two per week, an astounding quantity by all comparisons for the time! The four craftsmen, who were now employees of Pheneous through The Midas Touch Company, were thrilled. Pheneous' reaction was so joyous it was beyond description.

His company, the shares of which he and the four craftsmen held, was formed during the construction of the Pudding Engine and given its name because, unlike the hot pudding pot on the stove, the Pudding Engine could be touched.

The Midas Touch Company made huge profits during the next five years through its competitive edge over the other craftsmen. With all its disposable income, Pheneous thought the company should invest and diversify into other areas of production, the natural place to begin being other uses for the Pudding Engine. So the company began to make more Pudding Engines with different types of arm attachments to do different tasks – a custom-made product to suit each customer's need.

Pheneous soon discovered he could make a higher profit from manufacturing and selling Pudding Engines than from swords, so he phased out the sword line and sold his own Pudding Engine to the four struggling sword craftsmen.

The profit from the sale of a Pudding Engine was a thousand *pounds* or the equivalent of a thousand swords. The selling price itself was said by many to be a *King's ransom*, but if competitors were buying the engine, those who complained of the price had little choice. Pheneous held a monopoly.

Pheneous completed his report for the government claiming his solution to the problem of production meeting the pent-up demand created by *boodle*. The government was especially delighted with Midas because he had not only outlined the problem and the alternative courses of action, but he had actually built the solution. For this, they rewarded him by making him the first Honorary Knight, a reward which would be given, for centuries to follow, to those who fell into favour with the British Government.

Sir Pheneous *made his pile* from the Pudding Engine primarily because he held a monopoly in the market for many years – also a first for history.

One of Pheneous's first sales was to The Nimble Wood Joint Stock Company in 1766. Its founders and Erasmus Pelf were now dead and the operation was managed by new colonials. The company was engaged in a fierce competitive battle with four other saw mills at the time. And to win the economic battle, The Nimble Wood Joint Stock Company thought the Pudding Engine would give it the extra edge. Well, as it turned out, customers of lumber companies did not want an extra edge. They preferred regularly shaped products without the extra edge, so customers objected by not buying products from the company. And without sales, the company for the second time in its history could not generate sufficient funds to pay its debts. Eventually, its creditors were forced to commence legal action against the company which, in turn, led to a debtors' court hearing. The presiding judge reviewed all the evidence as well as the arguments presented by all parties. In its final brief, The Nimble Wood Joint Stock Company argued that excess competition caused the problem. But when all was heard, the judge concluded the issue was not competition. In his final decision, the judge admonished the shareholders of the company by stating, "You just didn't have the *Midas Touch*."

$ $ $ $ $ $

The Pudding Engine sales flourished and The Midas Touch Company was touted as a model capital company for more than one hundred years. Because of its inspiration, other engines and machines were invented and put into production, all increasing the speed at which other products were created. Sales could now be made at a quicker pace and, hence, *moullah* collected in larger quantities, also at a quicker pace. But the invention of such machines cost money because they required experiments, supplies and labour which, in turn, placed further pressure on the economy to employ more people.

By 1760, more than seven thousand people were employed by and earning wages from invention companies – all who would otherwise have had to seek employment elsewhere to acquire their *basic bread*; especially if the economic explosion to generate more money had not occurred. In other words, money when utilized to manufacture goods, generated greater amounts of money, a greater level of happiness for investors, inventors, employees and suppliers who, in turn, sold more goods and services to customers at a faster pace.

All the excess capital which existed during the late 1600's was now almost fully employed and working hard to create more. As demand was now being satisfied, entrepreneurs turned to new less costly ways to manufacture and deliver goods and services. And because the general demand for sales had now levelled and was not growing by greater rates, the only way to increase profit further was to reduce costs. Therefore, between 1750 and 1850 all new capital was directed toward improving the productivity of production and making obsolete that which had been created by previous capital.

This process of advancing the level of machine quality was driven purely by the desire to outperform competitors. The businessmen of the day certainly were not forward thinking enough to realize that building bigger or better Pudding Engines could possibly create new demands from old customers. When it did in spite of lack of foresight, society focused more on the problem of how to discard old or used machines than on rekindled sales and improved productivity. And, with necessity being the motherhood of profit, a whole new tier of business class became happier by selling used equipment to those who could not afford the latest models – more happy people and more profit. It was a strange phenomenon that someone could profit from the equipment from which others had already derived a profit. But that was capitalism in Europe.

$ $ $ $ $ $

While all this economic activity was going on in Europe and between the European countries and the Americas, China and Russia were not progressing quite as fast. The vast size of their countries and under-developed ports frustrated the advance of communication. And, because they had no interest in the New World, they did not share in the wealth and treasure which sparked the economic explosion in Europe. Moreover, these countries stuck to their ancient ways of making crafts on an individual basis, so people did not move close together to form economic units or companies in towns or major trade cities. So when travellers such as the Polo brothers journeyed to the Far East, they bought treasures from individual families in remote locations.

Also, Russia and China never moved from their strict rule by monarchy. There were no parliaments to focus upon the demands and needs of the people – to see to their advancement. Only the Czars and Kings advanced by hoarding their nations' treasures for themselves. They usually ruled by a divine power which, the people were told, was handed to them from ancient traditions or some sort of god. The peasant mentality persisted to the point where, because of their ignorance, the people of these countries had no motivation or knowledge to better themselves.

Once, a salesman from The Midas Touch Company met the Czar of Russia to discuss the sale of Pudding Engines for the industrialization of Russia. When the Czar demanded a special price for each machine, the salesman could only quote ten thousand *pounds* per unit.

"What?" yelled the Czar. "That's a *King's ransom*. In Russia, *money doesn't grow on trees*, you know!"

"Well, in Europe, such a sum is considered *pin money* or *chicken feed* now," responded the salesman.

"Maybe," said the Czar, "but your *pin money* isn't worth a *harp shilling* or a *nimble ninepence* here."

And with that, the salesman was thrown out of the country, leaving Russia destined to remain a second world nation for at least the next three hundred years.

Similar meetings were attempted with the rulers of China. However, the ways of the Chinese were simple: they ate, worshipped idols and smoked opium. There were plenty of rice fields to feed them, any old idol would do, and opium grew wild. So what could industrialized Europe offer the Chinese? When they were approached to buy the Pudding Engine, the effects of their opium habit made them laugh to the point of becoming hysterical. They thought the name of the apparatus was so stupid, it might as well be a giant cooking pot! So China, Russia and many other countries with the same attitude were meant to stand still economically for some time. The economic activity for the next three to four hundred years would be in the west, not the east.

The two countries did, however, create primitive currencies for peasant trading. In China, Emperor Chang Kai Wang was very fond of his mistress and successfully kept her identity from his wife for some twenty-five years. On their twenty-fifth non-anniversary, he minted a coin upon which he imprinted a picture of his wife on one side, and a picture of his mistress on the other – to symbolize the two-facedness of both the coin and his relationships. He christened the coin the *ywan*, which was an acronym of some sort from the last names of each of the two women.

In Russia, the Czar also minted a rudimentary coin during the early eighteen hundreds. He, however, did not have a mistress because he was a czar and no prince charming – and the Mongol women were large women and good only for moving furniture. Instead, the Czar's economy was in rubble, and not being very imaginative he simply called his coin rubble – or *rouble* as the Mongolians pronounced it.

$ $ $ $ $ $ $

During this time period in London, Desbois Able's circus was still travelling about the country performing for all those who had greater *disposable income*. The company was now owned and operated by Sir Sebastian Cabbage (1780 – 1860) who was a descendant of Desbois Able, twice removed.

Sir Sebastian Cabbage, by 1815, was moving the company throughout all the English colonies. He had been to India, Bermuda, Egypt and many others. Sir Sebastian certainly made the circus company international during his lifetime, which was far beyond Desbois Able's wildest dreams.

Now, old Cabbage knew the circus business well because he became the owner by working his way through every job in the company. He started out with a monkey, teaching him new tricks so people would drop more money into its cup. The monkey had to work harder to attract more money or Sebastian would have cut it from the list of acts. Before it was Sebastian's responsibility, the monkey was lazy and only attracted pittance. And a *monkey's pittance* was not even enough to pay for the food it ate – that is, its *basic bread*. Sebastian didn't stand for such monkey business.

Once Sir Sebastian Cabbage was through with the monkey, people in the circus referred to *monkey's pittance* as money related to very hard work – or increased productivity. Before long, all the circus people were earning a *monkey's pittance* as Sir Sebastian Cabbage forced increased human productivity from every job in the company. The increased productivity was the same as money in the bank. When people worked hard and performed more acts in less time, they brought in greater amounts of *moullah*. And, since

Cabbage paid a fixed wage to all, additional *pounds* earned became profit to him at no cost. When Sebastian documented this theory he, like Pheneous Midas, was knighted for his contribution to the enhancement of a *monkey's pittance.*

Once Sebastian was knighted, he planned to take the company to Egypt to perform for the King, but the engagement was cancelled because the King had been kidnapped and was being held for ransom. From the last contact with the authorities in Egypt, Sir Sebastian learned they were still bartering over the ransom price. So Cabbage turned his planning sights to the Americas.

The United States were now in their embryonic stage of formation. They had had their war of independence with Britain – obtaining the right to govern for themselves. They had also weathered a civil war – that is, if one may term any war as being civil. But these wars were expensive and somewhat counter-productive for a new country which needed every *harp shilling* to build its economic and social foundation.

Sir Sebastian Cabbage read the accounts of the new world development in the London papers. By 1825, he was reading about other battles between the United States Cavalry and the original natives, or Indians as they were called. It all sounded very exciting to him, so he wrote President Ulysses S. Grant of the United States asking if his company could visit to perform for him and other people across the United States. Cabbage included a fee schedule for President Grant to consider. A month later he received an invitation from the President to visit the United States. President Grant's letter, however, noted the cost in the fee schedule as being substantial and approaching a *King's ransom.*

Said the President in his letter, "I hope that you will take consideration of the fact that the *reign of ransom* has ended these twenty years. And, that the reign, these last three hundred years, has never fallen upon the United States of America."

6

Wild *Wampum*

While Europe had financially developed in a substantial way by 1825, the New World had also created some of its own money history. Serious financial developments in the New World really began around the year 1500.

By the mid 1500's, the financial and economic focus of all Europe was on the Americas which really included what was to become North America, as well as the Caribbean Islands. It was an exciting time for many people who chose the brave New World with the hopes and dreams of bettering their lot in life – especially those with two daughters.

Throughout the next three hundred years, the world focused little on the Middle and Far East from whence the likes of Moses Moullah, Barticus and the Polo brothers began the money process. They stood still economically, choosing to maintain variations of the feudal and tribal systems which cherished only historical events and idols. Their peoples were not future-oriented, nor did they possess the education, energy and inclination to pursue New Worlds. The tribes remained fragmented and concentrated more on fighting one another than on bettering themselves financially – with the result that they continued to be poor, living only at a subsistence level. They never knew the economic and psychological renewal experienced by the Western Europeans from the wealth and decadence generated by exploring the New World.

The Middle East fell farther behind economically by maintaining its extensive religious wars. The peoples in those countries were certainly less happy than those of Western Europe. They were always striving for some religious principle resulting in no money being earned to enjoy the pleasures of life. And, because watching the development of money, and its effects upon people's lives, is of primary interest here, one may be pardoned if one chooses to ignore those who follow the economic footsteps of China and Russia by standing still. One must return to the New World.

Since the history of Europe had already developed towns and cities to improve markets, mercantile activity and communication, the concept only had to be replicated in the Americas. Jamestown, New York and Philadelphia were among the first towns to develop in the late 1500's. Boston was also among the thriving centres. All were economic beehives and their growth and development was solely attributed to the creation of greater wealth and money, both for those who lived there and for those in Europe who financed their adventures.

The port towns of New York and Boston grew faster because of their proximity to Europe. The shipping companies sailed to these ports to load their precious cargoes for return to London, Paris and Lisbon. Thousands of people were employed and earned wages, on both sides of the Atlantic, while maintaining this activity.

During the early 1600's, New York was experiencing a construction boom. All the people required to work for the trading system had to live somewhere – and because of trade they now earned more money and could afford the better life style to which they had always aspired back in their native homelands. The construction boom created many beautiful mansions while it employed a substantial number of carpenters and stone masons who had moved from Europe. Now, a master craftsman was paid a lot more money for his work in America than he had earned in Europe. Everyone seemed to possess more money. Obtaining higher wages did not seem to be a problem – everyone was happier because their pockets were filled with more *moullah* than just *pin money*.

New York became a melting pot for Europeans. While the homeland people of England were bitterly racing both the Dutch and French to acquire the largest piece of the Americas, the new generation of people from all three countries were living side by side in New York – becoming a new and united people. The new generation was creating so much wealth together it made no sense to draw artificial national boundaries among themselves – just in the name of bitterness among their forefathers.

Wall Street's primary purpose was to keep thieves out – a purpose that could reverse itself over time

Since money had brought greater comfort than had been experienced in home countries, it wasn't long before the people used that money to found all the cornerstones of their homeland culture. It came as no surprise to find that one of these cornerstones was the church. After all, history has shown that where money and wealth were developed at a great rate, the church was not far behind. And so, in 1697, Trinity Church was built in New York and proceeded to become the most fashionable place to be seen Sundays, at least before the American revolution.

Life, however, was not without some hardship. The lives of the settlers were constantly being threatened by native Indians. They were considered savages because of their dress – or lack of it – and their thirst for blood and whiskey. They frequently raided New York, killing all those in sight and stealing whiskey, flour and other goods in order to feed themselves. They had no money, nor did they know what it was, or how to use it. The Indians survived by either *bartering* or taking provisions by force. It was almost as if time had stood still for these people from the days of Barticus.

The Indians around New York were led by a particularly tough and legendary chief, Chief Little Dole (1623 – 1723). Now Little

Dole looked upon New York as a source of supply, and with three thousand braves to feed, he was fortunate to have a town the size of New York. At first, Little Dole and his braves would only raid the town periodically, but as his standard of living grew along with tribal pressures to have all the modern conveniences, he began a regular weekly run – usually during Saturday night.

Now this common problem brought the settlers, from all countries, closer together and accelerated the election of town councils and an area governor. They fussed over the title of "governor" because of its biblical connotation of corruption and poor fiscal management. However, no one could think of a better title, so they chose to ignore the history of Governor General Light.

The first order of duty for these elected officials was to rid the New York area of the Indians in general, and their chief, Chief Little Dole specifically. In 1653, the Governor ordered the construction of a wall made of thick planks between the Hudson and East Rivers on the west side of the outer street. Wall Street, as it was named, was the front for the Indian raids and existed solely to keep out renegades. The Governor didn't foresee that many years later renegades would also be found on the east side of Wall Street.

Wall Street held off Chief Little Dole for a short period of time, but the Chief, who was scratching for provisions, was just itching to break down the neighbourhood barrier. Now, as history would have it, Little Dole had an ally in not only his own greed, but also in the greed of the white man. The settlers themselves stole the planks from the wall to build their houses or for firewood during the winter. This left the town exposed again and Little Dole resumed his Saturday night raids.

Throughout 1655, Chief Little Dole successfully "wamped" the white man every Saturday night, taking all the goods and provisions required to maintain his tribe. The Chief and his warriors got drunk after raiding the taverns, shot up the town and raped the cattle, then they left in peace. The following Saturday night the process was repeated again with the commencement of "Let's Wamp'em" from Chief Little Dole. It was wild and the settlers associated this cry with the commencement yell of a wild Saturday night when everyone let loose. They budgeted for extra provisions to be stolen by the Indians which, oddly enough, became the forerunner of the first welfare system. So with time, Chief Little

Dole didn't have to use force to satisfy his needs. In actual fact, the locals gathered on Wall Street at sundown on Saturday night to yell, "Wild Wamp'em" before Little Dole could get the now largely ceremonial words out. The words became generic for letting off steam or frustration. But, in the white man's world, it cost money to have a wild Saturday night – money which had to be set aside from their *basic bread* to become the separate household budget item – *wild wampum*.

$$\$\,\$\,\$\,\$\,\$\,\$\,\$$$

Now that Chief Little Dole was basically accepted, or at least tolerated by New Yorkers, he became more tame. He learned English and was tutored by his daughter Pretty Penny who went to school in the town. He was legendary as the town character, still maintaining his *wild wampum* night – the difference being that by 1675 he was actually earning wages as a shop-keeper in a shop owned by a wealthy merchant. Now, he earned his *wild wampum* honestly and paid for his own food and drink from his earnings. This life, however, was not for his tribe. They liked the traditional beliefs of "Wamp'em" and soon became disenchanted with Dole's following of the white man's ways. By 1680, all his warriors had left, moving west to the new frontiers and new settlers to wamp.

By 1683, Chief Little Dole was borderline respectable – at least enough to be encouraged to run for town council. This he did on the platform of developing an organized welfare system, a policy of which he had been credited for previously through his wild raids for provisions. He won a seat easily during the 1683 fall elections.

During the council debate in 1684, Councilman Dole persuaded his fellow members to vote in favour of a Bill creating the Welfare Incentive Programme (WIP), a central agency empowered to give away ten percent of the town's annual funds to the poor.

Now no one at the time realized the tremendous potential monetary impact of this program. First, money which would otherwise be deployed to develop a larger, stronger economy was now being given away for no consideration. And, those who were borderline lazy now could apply for a "WIPing" and enjoy it while not contributing anything to the town's productivity whatsoever. A drop in productivity, together with the giving of town funds, had a double-barrelled effect on the local economy. So, economic activity slowed down during 1685–86, becoming sluggish and lack-lustre in performance.

Moreover, there was a psychological effect upon the people who got "WIPed". They were embarrassed to be living off their fellow man and contributing nothing in return. A welfare official visited these people weekly, sometimes delivering a few *shillings*, and sometimes *pelf*, a local currency which filtered into town through the workers of The Nimble Wood Joint Stock Company. But, to those who received a "WIPing", it would always be called *dole* or *scratch*. And not only did it bear the name of Chief Little Dole, its creator, but it also symbolized hard times and the necessity to scratch even for *pin money* or a *nimble ninepence*. The lack of earned money made the people unhappy, and many turned to a life of evil and crime just for something to do.

The town now had a problem with productivity, crime, ineffective spending and morale – all because an old savage wanted to do good. Needless to say, Chief Little Dole was voted out of office in 1688 and a new council set out to fix the problem.

But trying to fix the system and right wrong was not so easy. Even though morale was low, people were, in fact, receiving money for nothing – and once given the privilege, it was virtually impossible to take it away. So the city had an economic structural problem because handouts lessened morale, but not handing out lessened morale more.

Moreover, employees and entrepreneurs were forced to compensate for the lost productivity through the purchase and deployment of black slaves from the South or the African boats. This, in turn, meant a double cost to the system because local people were paid not to work and, at the same time, foreign people were purchased to complete the same work. It was all quite silly when properly analyzed. It was even more silly one hundred years later when the uneducated slaves were freed, couldn't find employment and, hence, increased the numbers on the *dole*. That's right, one hundred years later the townspeople were being taxed to pay *dole* or *scratch* to people they had already bought to eliminate the financial effects of *dole* in the first place – not a very logical system. In fact, it served to be inflationary, with the cost of slaves lost and taxes increased to pay the ever increasing expense of *dole*. And prior to the freedom of the slaves, *dole* had increased to eleven per cent of the town budget.

$ $ $ $ $ $ $

When Chief Little Dole was defeated during the election of 1688, he and a German friend, Henry Thaler, spent *wild wampum* for a week. When they finally sobered up, they discovered they both had lost their jobs. And being in need of work, they visited the management of The Nimble Wood Joint Stock Company seeking employment. Thaler had met Erasmus Pelf once before he was killed by Francis the Torturer, and he used this bit of useless social history to secure employment for himself and Dole at the mill. There, they worked until 1690.

They became friends with Erasmus Pelf Jr., who, on many occasions, recounted the history of The Nimble Wood Joint Stock Company and its founders, Woody Barker, Jack Nimble and Francis the Torturer. Dole and Thaler not only learned a lot about the lumber business, but also how Erasmus Pelf Sr. had created his own currency to take over the American operation. They discovered that the word "bark" for the outer part of trees, and the term "wood" for the cut pieces they felled were both derivatives of Woody Barker's name. Some of the company products and processes were also permanent monuments to its three original founders The term "plywood" for one of their products represented pliable or nimble wood after Jack Nimble. And "pressure treated wood" was reflective of Francis the Torturer's management style.

Life was peaceful for Chief Little Dole and Henry Thaler during the two years they worked at the Mill. Henry, in fact, fell in love with Dole's daughter, Pretty Penny. They married in 1689 and had a baby boy in 1690 whom they named Small Change. The marriage and the baby brought Dole and Thaler even closer together. Many evenings over a few beers they talked of starting their own business. Dreams of creating a currency like *pelf* were frequently a part of their smoozing.

Both had too much entrepreneurial blood in them to be happy continuing as labourers at the mill. So, in 1691, they all moved back to New York, pooled their money and bought a small boarding house. Once they had moved in, Henry Thaler immediately raised the room prices and fired two cleaning staff, replacing them with Pretty Penny, all to increase the family's *wild wampum.*

Chief Little Dole visited all his old friends who, to his amazement, were pushing him to run again for town council. Dole resisted because of his age and his feeling that the people would never re-elect him. But his friends were persistent, declaring that all he had to do was to develop a political platform and his charisma would do the rest. So, as with everything, he talked the matter over with his confidant and friend – Henry Thaler. Henry thought Dole could win a seat again but only if it was on a platform of monetary and fiscal issues.

Dole thought about what would happen if he created a new town currency to replace *pelf* and *pounds*. It would appeal to the national feeling of the colonists who were beginning to begrudge the British the profit they were reaping from the colonies. It would also eliminate the confusion of having two currencies in one town causing a constant exchange problem on a daily basis. Thaler thought the idea was great and volunteered himself as Dole's campaign manager and monetary advisor. And, in order to appear effective and knowledgeable, they read the history of Moses Moullah, Plutomania, Lirabus and others.

When they had researched the subject to their liking, they decided upon a coin which they created together, and therefore, named jointly – the "Dolehaler" – pronounced *dollar*. The *dollar*, if mass-produced, would be exchanged one for each British *pound*, but it would require ten *pelf coins* to be turned in for the same exchange. The two would-be politicians knew the latter ratio would cause problems with certain voters.

Nevertheless, Chief Little Dole threw his hat into the political ring once again during 1693, using the *dollar* as both his platform and his source to finance it. When the ballots were all cast, Dole received 51% of the votes while his single anti-*dollar* opponent secured 49%. Oddly enough, the vote, split between the two political opponents, approximated the circulation of the *pound* versus the *pelf*. In any case, Dole placed his *dollar* Bill before the new town council and it passed the member vote by 51% to 49% – the *dollar* had been created by New York!

$ $ $ $ $ $ $

By 1695 the *dollar* had replaced all remaining units of the two other currencies. The average weekly wage in New York at this time was ten *dollars* and a typical family budget was something like the following:

- *basic bread* (food, clothing, shelter) $4.00
- *pin money* (sewing, furniture, household utensils)   2.00

• tithes and taxes (church, city)	1.00
• *wild wampum* (Saturday night drink)	2.00
• *widow's mite* (money held by wife as security in case of husband's death)	<u>1.00</u>
TOTAL FAMILY BUDGET	<u>$10.00</u>

Widow's mite was really money controlled by the woman of the family as was the case in the time of Jesus. It became savings to be used by the family in case the *basic bread* winner lost his job or was unable to work for some reason or another. It was also the first *dollar* to be taken each Saturday from the family coffers, so it did not accidentally form part of the *wild wampum budget* that night. As wives were religious about taking their *widow's mite*, the amounts grew to large sums by the time the *bread* winner reached retirement. The funds were then used to finance their senior years. During these times, the home and family were often referred to as the "nest", an analogy taken from the life of the great American eagle. So it followed that the growth in the amount of *widow's mite* to finance the nest during retirement years became known as the *nest egg* – more so than *widow's mite*.

$ $ $ $ $ $ $

Now, by the early 1700's, *wild wampum* was beginning to have a strange effect on the economy. To accommodate consumer demand for wild nights and the spending of *wild wampum,* taverns sprung up all over New York. Prostitution and gambling grew and flourished during the first twenty-five years of the new century. As a matter of fact, it very much resembled Sodom and Gomorrah.

But no matter how bad things got, Chief Little Dole was not above seizing an opportunity to earn more *dollars*. And, at the age of ninety-six, he and Thaler sold the rooming house for a tidy sum – which was to be anointed as a *pretty penny* in honour of Dole's daughter and Thaler's wife who had worked extremely hard managing the house for the past twenty-eight years. But Pretty Penny never saw a *penny*. The two old cronies used the tidy sum to build a tavern during the summer of 1719. In search of a name for the tavern, they went back in time to their days at The Nimble Wood Joint Stock Company and the stories of its founders. Dole was always moved by Francis the Torturer, perhaps because the savage nature of the man reminded the Chief of himself in his younger days. So the two agreed to call the new establishment 'Francis

Tavern' in honour of one of the first entrepreneurs in America. The tavern was extremely successful but only Henry Thaler and Pretty Penny lived to see it earn its *loaves and fishes* throughout the first ten years of operation.

Chief Little Dole died in 1723 and was given a royal funeral by the town he once terrorized and later almost destroyed economically. But in the final analysis, he finally gave the *dollar* to Wall Street and the people were grateful for this. Henry Thaler and his wife eventually sold the tavern, again for another *pretty penny* which they kept for their *nest egg*.

$ $ $ $ $ $ $

Throughout the 1700's, towns similar to New York developed from the Atlantic Seaboard to the Pacific Ocean. New York became the gateway to these cities and the corridor for trade with new settlers from Europe. Many people worked in New York for a couple of years to save a *nest egg* of *dollars* large enough to move west – with the net result of the *dollar* coin spreading throughout the central part of what was now North America by 1760. The northern part of the continent, however, remained loyal to the British *pound* and maintained closer ties with London.

London was becoming somewhat distraught with the colonists because of their growing desire to control their own destiny. Many territories in America were still governed, at great expense, by London or Paris. The people in the New World had no say in their own government as it was administered with no representation. In addition, the pedantic British nose was slightly out of joint at the thought of their *pound* not being widely accepted in the New World. All this caused friction between the colonists and the British – friction which grew to the point of fighting during the late 1760's.

What followed was to become the American Revolution, a fierce and vicious fight between the colonists for self-government and the British for maintaining their control. It absorbed a tremendous amount of money on both sides – more so for the British because of their travelling expenses to fight on foreign soil. But at least the British had the *pounds* to lose. The colonists, on the other hand, were quite financially thin. All they had was the *dollar* as a localized currency and that wasn't yet minted nationally by any country. So frequently the colonists' army went unpaid for their services, but the fire in their bellies more than offset the extra *pounds* the British carried around. Besides, the British didn't really have their heart in the exercise because the fight wasn't on British soil. Thus the colonists won, declaring independence in 1776.

The first continental congress was held in 1774 and was attended by the man who would later lead the country to victory – George Washington. One might say the British helped form the first government by forcing the colonists to organize and fight – the very thing they were trying to prevent. Nevertheless the musket smoke finally cleared and the British realized they had mastered their own loss.

It wasn't until the early 1780's that the last of the loyalists had either returned to Britain or moved north. And during this period, George Washington, Thomas Jefferson, James Madison and James Munro drafted a constitution, procedures of government and a financial structure which, unbeknownst to them, would guide the new United States to world economic and military power during the next two hundred years.

The financial structure included an assumption, by a new Federal Government, of all individual state debts created during the revolution. George Washington became the first President in 1789, and his treasurer, Alexander Hamilton, refinanced these state debts through the Federal Government – thereby relieving the states of their financial burdens. Hamilton also created a National Federal Bank so the country could transact in bonds, notes and deposits. And although the *dollar* was inflated and suffered a beating during the revolution, it did survive and, hence, deserved some loyalty as far as Hamilton was concerned. So it was adopted as the official currency of the United States, and was finally minted nationally during 1793.

Of course the government itself required *dollars* to operate and was forced to adopt the older countries' ancient systems of tithes and taxes, modified slightly from church experience and local, down-home input. An easy target for a new tax was against *wild wampum*, primarily because it was spent in such great quantities and did not seem to interfere with the *basic bread* of the population. Now, having no prior experience in taxation matters, Washington and Hamilton went a little overboard when it came to *wild wampum*. The tax on this service item led to the "whiskey rebellion" of 1794.[39] The rebellion forced an easing of taxation on

---

[39] Profiles and Portraits of American Presidents and their Wives, Chapter 1, Page 2

wild wampum for whiskey because this money really made people happy. And although the effects of excess whiskey could be evil, the money used to buy it represented disposable income – and to have it taxed would mean it would no longer be disposable.

The United States grew quickly during the first hundred years, acquiring new states, paying off revolutionary debts, and generally making treaties around the world to have itself recognized. The people kept the feeling of freedom, experienced during the revolution, alive with spirit and celebration. There was an underlying *esprit de corps* which filled everyone's chest with pride. They had conquered Britain, the then world power, instantly creating a national ego with a tremendous appetite – an appetite which if not fed, created morale deflation and a feeling of just being average.

Now, with human nature being what it is, once a feeling of above-average is attained, anything less just seems to lead to poor performance regardless of the task considered. So when the Americans did not feel superior, emotional decay set in bringing lower productivity, higher unemployment and, hence, poorer financial performance for the country. The concepts of competition, jealousy and revenge, created by God during *Biblical Barter, Part I,* became the root of this behaviour. It created a culture built upon the internal feeling that Americans and the United States were never supposed to lose. And, as with all egomaniacs, this attitude caused an inward self-focus and the beginning of the isolation policy for the country. It was not observed at the time, nor would it have been socially acceptable to do so, that this self-centred dream would create a great financial and political empire based upon expectations – expectations which one day might not be fulfilled. The expectation that wealth, fame, fortune and glory were always around the corner was embedded in the American people as much as, or more than, the Constitution.

Competition and the freedom to compete became the national theme. As time would have it, competition grew both internally and with other countries. New ways to maintain superiority forced people to draw upon the other basic personal traits, given by God, such as evil, negotiation, killing, anger, reneging on agreements and promiscuity. *Wild wampum* was often used to buy these traits, resulting in people making money and accumulating wealth from selling their basic God-given characteristics – all to maintain some level of superiority. But, as the nation was growing and cities and industries developing, no one gave any thought to there being a fine line between superiority and inferiority.

$ $ $ $ $ $ $

Not all the growth within the United States during the 1800's came easily. Although the "Let's wamp'em" Indians moved further west with time, so did the white man's walls. The Indian wars lasted many years with the surviving savages being given tracts of land known as reservations. The white man's conscience was such that the Indians had to be given something in return for having their land taken. So they received pieces of desert free and access to the federal *dole* system, which had been adopted across the country from New York. Interestingly enough, when Chief Little Dole developed the system of *scratch*, he didn't realize that one hundred years later his own people would become the main recipient of the same, but nationalized plan! That's right. Many of the descendants of Little Dole's raiding warriors were now receiving their *wild wampum,* compliments of the United States Government and without any raiding requirements.

The most unfortunate outcome was that *dole* had the same affect on the Indians as it did on the white man. No self-respect was maintained because their livelihood was taken from them, and there was no reason to be productive as long as the white man provided them with *dole*. And because they were isolated on reservations from the rest of society, they could never hope to better themselves. This became the attitude which most adopted, causing a self-perpetuating separate lower class without the spirit or the will to become anything else. To them, isolation from mainstream United States, prejudice, lack of motivation and education, and low self-esteem were the root of all evil – an evil which could have been eliminated if they had been recognized as Americans, permitted to live and work anywhere, and earned money in exchange for labour supplied.

Chief Little Dole himself accomplished all this one hundred years prior to the creation of reservations. But then the warriors deserted him, because of his pro-white man politics, to continue with their savage raids. As society would have it, the physical abuse inflicted by the Indians was to be retaliated against by the white man's psychological abuse. One wonders how the two approaches compare in God's eyes.

$ $ $ $ $ $ $

By 1825, America was known as the land of big spenders. Everything was conducted in an ostentatious style compared with that of the forefathers in Europe. When companies were organized they were large; when parties were held they were large; when money was made and lost it was in large quantities. And when revenge was taken, it was really taken. The world was seeing those original traits, instilled in mankind by God, used in a truly magnificent style.

The greatest display of decadence took place in 1826 when President Grant engaged Sir Sebastian Cabbage and his circus to come to Washington to perform. Three hundred and fifty circus people landed in Washington on September 6, 1826, at a cost of $10,000 to the United States government. People came from all over the United States to see this circus and Washington was bustling with people. There were no hotel rooms left to rent for the whole of the two months the show was in town. Everyone was drunk and spending more *wild wampum* than budgeted. There was one continuous party twenty-four hours a day. It was a real circus!

The President held a state dinner in honour of Sir Sebastian Cabbage, and it was rumoured that dinner cost more than a *monkey's pittance*. There was live entertainment during the dinner which included singing, dancing and juggling. In actual fact, President Grant held a circus to honour a circus – perhaps the American competition and superiority creeping in from what otherwise would have been a normal diplomatic dinner.

For the two months the circus ran in Washington, some two hundred thousand people visited it for entertainment. People got so carried away with the spending of *wild wampum* that they actually borrowed money to stay the two months. But once they borrowed *wild wampum*, it automatically became *basic bread* because it had to be repaid – that is, repayment was a necessity.

Meanwhile, Sir Sebastian was becoming a millionaire through the money the Americans were spending. He deposited all his profits in a bank in New York for safe-keeping. The tellers there were so used to his huge weekly deposits that when they saw him coming one would say: "Here comes a new *pile of cabbage*". *Cabbage* became the new slang word, among bankers in New York, for excess profits. But because Sir Sebastian was both

Sir Sebastian Cabbage watches the American people turn his cabbage *into* spinach, *and then* gravy

winning and British, it was not considered right for him to be profiting from the American system.

To further aggravate Cabbage's American associates, Sir Sebastian complained about how little he was earning for the number of circus people he had to feed and clothe – 'poor-mouthing' as the Americans called it. Such poor-mouthing went on while Sir Sebastian *would cry all the way to the bank*. And he had taken so much *moullah* from their pockets he was beyond *cabbage* – he was now into *spinach* and *gravy*.

People now had some guideline as to what might be normal excessive profit – *cabbage*; perfect excessive profit – *spinach*; and the pluperfect of excessive profit – *gravy*. Because Washington had generated real *gravy* for Sir Sebastian, he decided he liked the United States very much. So he thought he might move the circus around a bit and generate a *king's ransom*.

After a month of travel, the caravan decided to set up for an additional two-month period in the city of Chicago. But here, Cabbage ran into something he had never encountered before – political opposition. It appeared the city council did not want the circus to extract enormous amounts of wealth, which would otherwise have been available for taxation, from its people. The city money, or purse as it was called, could not afford the same run as Washington suffered. The purse was running low on its reserve of money and an increase in tax was being contemplated.

Sir Sebastian approached the town council and offered the city $15,000 in exchange for a two-month circus permit. Now, even in 1827 this amount wasn't *chicken feed*. It was a substantial amount of *script* to anyone's pocketbook. The council turned it down as being unethical to accept. However, Sir Sebastian did not waver in his determination.

One night someone visited the mayor's yacht, moored off the south shore, and left $15,000 in the ship's ammunition locker. Two days later Cabbage received his circus permit. But when he was setting up the circus one afternoon, the mayor appeared and wondered aloud.

"See you finally received your circus permit, Sir Sebastian. I suppose this will enable you to earn a *pretty penny* and continue you on your way to becoming a man of means."

"Well, Your Worship," replied Cabbage with a grin, "you might say it is equivalent to a *shot in the locker*."

Nothing more was ever said between the two, but this exchange was believed to be the first recorded bribe of any substance.

Nevertheless, the good people of Chicago got to spend their *wild wampum* and, indeed, part of their *nest eggs*. They came out of the hills of Illinois to spend their *dollars* as if *money burned a hole in one's pocket*. Everyone seemed determined to give Sir Sebastian Cabbage his *shot in the locker*.

Handling considerable sums of money was now physically a lot easier since the government began printing paper *dollar bills*. Coins or *bullion* were heavy and difficult to transport. *Bills*, on the other hand, could be concealed on the person, stored in secret locations and were not prone to noise when accidentally bumped together. Husbands could quietly sneak extra *wild wampum* from their savings jars and wives could bosom extra *pin money*. Generally, paper *dollars*, or *greenbacks* as they were called, made covert financial activity more efficient and quiet, and without the need for extra manpower to move it.

Sir Sebastian Cabbage travelled to all the major American cities during the next five years, bringing joy and happiness to children in exchange for their parents' *wild wampum*. But because

Ces Poole argues for the honour of wild wampum *and for Sebastian Cabbage*

the Americans spent money in large quantities, the circus had the effect of creating inflation to, at least, the *wild wampum* portion of the family budget. The *nest egg* was the first to feel the pinch because the *basic bread* was basically sacred. When the American people finally realized their savings were all going to a British entertainment company, they charged Sir Sebastian with organizing an economic coup on behalf of the British government. He was charged with treason in 1832 amidst protests from the British government.

At his trial he was represented by a clever young lawyer named Cecil Poole. The hearing began in San Francisco on October 12, 1832. Once the prosecution had finished with its case against Cabbage for malicious economic acts against the United States of America, Ces Poole rose to his feet.

"Your Honour, have you ever attended Sir Sebastian Cabbage's circus?"

"Yes, I have – took my children there," replied the judge.

"Did you have a good time?"

"Yes!"

"Objection, Your Honour," snapped the prosecutor. "Is Mr. Poole going to call you as a witness?"

"No, it would not be proper court procedure to do so," ruled the judge.

"Your Honour, it is not my intention to call you as a witness, but it is important to my client's defence to demonstrate to the court what pleasure his business provides the community," exclaimed Poole.

"Proceed!" snapped the judge.

"Now, Your Honour, are you like the rest of us? Do you have a budget for a little *wild wampum* which you use for family or personal fun?" asked Poole.

"Yes, I do."

"And do you spend that money according to your own desire; that is, your needs and pleasures?"

"Yes, I do."

"No one, Your Honour, has ever told you how to spend your *wild wampum* generally, or specifically in this case, not to spend it at the circus?"

"No, they haven't. It would be against the Constitution," replied the judge.

"Right."

"Now then, suppose, Your Honour, that you wished to increase the amount of your *wild wampum,* thereby reducing your *nest egg.* That would be a decision between you and your wife, would it not?"

"Yes, of course. This is a ridiculous line of questioning. And I won't tolerate it much longer in my court," growled the Judge.

"I beg the indulgence of the court," pleaded Poole. "I won't be much longer."

"Proceed."

"What you're saying to me, Your Honour, is that Sir Sebastian Cabbage, my client, did not control your spending of *wild wampum* in any way or in any quantity," pronounced Poole.

"No, nor would it have been logical to do so. *Wild wampum* is called so because it is wild spending, and wild spending is not, by definition, controllable," ruled the judge.

"Defence moves to have all charges against Sir Sebastian Cabbage dropped on the basis of the authoritative rulings by Your Honour," stated Ces Poole triumphantly.

"So ordered," stated the judge, scratching his head. "*Wild wampum* has always been the root of all happiness for my family."

7

Bad *Boodle* or Conspicuous *Cabbage*?

When Sir Sebastian Cabbage was tried for treason in 1832, Chester Alan Arthur was President of the United States. Prosperity continued as new frontiers moved further west, albeit the prosperity was in the hands of a few. The majority of the population was still very close to earning only *basic bread* with a little disposable income on the side. Most surplus *dollars*, however, were in the hands of the few well-developed New England states and among the big ranches of Texas.

Wealth in the hands of a few within a growing struggling nation, together with the added humiliation of *dole*, created a not-so-pleasant phenomenon – more crime. People became lodged in certain lower classes, and without money they could not gain higher levels of education and social grace or standing. And without such education and social grace they could not acquire employment to earn more money. The result was widespread depression.

Among the poorer class, though, were militant union or guild leaders who, because of their descendence from Moabites and Ammonites, acted somewhat irrationally. They recruited all the independent thieves and unemployables into an organized unit against decent society – a form of radical protest against the 'haves' by the 'havenots'.

The primary organizer of the 'havenots' was John T. Boodle V (1850 – 1915), a Chicago bully cum hoodlum. He was, nevertheless, a forceful speaker with persuasive techniques somewhat similar to those of Francis the Torturer. John T. was quite wealthy in his own right, being left a considerable sum of *boodle* by his great

great grandfather, of the same name, who lived in the Caribbean. People were always suspicious of the source of Boodle's wealth, but none dared to question him on the matter.

Now, by 1890, John T. Boodle V had modelled his organization of otherwise useless people along the lines of modern corporations which were developing in the United States. He, of course, was president and had appointed a number of undistinguished vice-presidents with the following functional responsibilities:

Hy Solitude	Drug Trafficking
Lo Ki	Protectionism
Denny Dinero	Counterfeit Money
Gung Ho	Arms Sales
J.J. Hooker	Prostitution

Solitude was always high with his friends, and led a rather lonely life compared with his associates. He was known to be somewhat manic-depressive, a condition considered by those around him as one of the hazards of his job.

Lo Ki was the vice-president who worked more effectively by not attracting public attention. He built a profitable division by moving quietly through the business districts, gently offering protection in situations where the police force seemed to be ineffective. To be high profile was not considered a Lo Ki management style.

Denny Dinero was the illegitimate son of an Iowa pig farmer, and was raised on the fat of the land. Although he lived high on the hog, the good life was taken from him suddenly when all his father's pigs had to be shot because of disease. His father was forced to declare bankruptcy as a result and the family was destined to be penniless thereafter. Dinero was bitter about this past but found some comfort in religion. As he was of Italian descent, it was natural that he became an Orthodox Jew. This served two needs – he did not have to eat any pork, a food which he singled out as the cause of his poverty, and he developed a God-given ability to make money – hence, his qualifications for vice-president of counterfeit money.

Gung Ho was an over anxious trigger-happy son of two Chinese restaurant owners from San Francisco. He was hospitalized on two occasions for anxiety due to imagining armed gang attacks. His nightmares made life intolerable and were the source of great research for psychiatrists. His nightmares of attacks against

John T. Boodle V discusses the performance of his company's divisions with his vice-presidents

him caused his anxiety level to reach extreme proportions, resulting occasionally in convulsions. This condition made the aiming of a gun somewhat difficult. But, he took some satisfaction that he, through his condition, indirectly assisted the medical profession discover "the anxiety attack."

J.J. Hooker was the descendant of a long line of Hookers, making him a natural leader for the prostitution division. His hereditary ability to live with hooking was nurtured by his mother. She taught him all the 'tricks' of the trade, as well as how to maximize profit from inventory. J.J. was truly made in his mother's image.

Now these five vice-presidents reported directly to John Boodle whose corporate philosophy was one of maximum functional synergy – that is, everyone works together for the benefit of the overall corporation, not just their separate divisions. This was not always easy but, thanks to Boodle's detailed organization approach, every area where one division could complement another was explored through strategic planning. This resulted in the formation of several economic 'food chains' to increase revenue.

For example, Hy Solitude's group sold drugs to certain low

life who did not meet the strict employment criteria to join the Chicago corporation. The customers, while high on drugs, would rob the local merchants to steal sufficient money to buy more drugs. Lo Ki would then sell a protectionist policy to the shopkeepers, supplying the manpower to minimize the attacks from drug addicts. Ki had to be careful though, as the addicts had to receive some funds. Otherwise Solitude's sales would decline and, in turn, there would be less need for protection – a double negative affect on the corporation's revenue.

The wealthy store owners were also encouraged to help with their own protection and were given certain protection policy discounts if they bought arms from Gung Ho's division salesmen.

All this activity was frequently too stressful for the wealthy shopkeepers, and so they often spent their *wild wampum* on J.J. Hooker's prostitutes for relief of stress.

Denny Dinero was good at making money which was issued to the staff to purchase goods and services for their own use. All employees were taught the difference between John T's *bad boodle dollar* and the government's *dollar*. To maximize profit, all revenues were to be collected in Government issue and all expenses were to be paid in *bad boodle*. So the arms dealers, prostitutes, drug salesmen and protectionists all had regular staff training meetings to ensure quality control, and that collections did not come in the form of Denny Dinero's *bad boodle* – a total all-in-one service package approach to extorting money from the rich to benefit the poor. In other words, a form of redistribution of wealth not dissimilar to that used by Robin Hood. In actual fact, the employees of John T. Boodle's corporation were frequently referred to as hoods.

It is important to note here that, in keeping with the corporation's strategic plan, no taxes were paid to the government on profits earned from the five divisions. This, of course, did not make the government happy but, in the absence of reliable evidence and stronger laws, the government did not take steps to collect – and if it had, in all likelihood it would have been paid in *bad boodle*!

The system worked well for John T. Boodle until approximately 1900. Until then, Boodle had a monopoly on organized crime in the United States. He could charge whatever he liked for the corporation's services and there was nothing the customers could do – there was no alternative source or competition.

John T. Boodle V is questioned on issuance of inconspicuous cabbage

However, by the turn of the century, another organization had been formed in Los Angeles, under the leadership of Leonard Cabbage – grandson of Sir Sebastian Cabbage.

Leonard's organization was originally based on counterfeit money. It perfected this commodity when it stole the government's *dollar* plates or moulds, duplicated them, and then returned the original plates without being noticed. Cabbage printed a million *dollars* in what was excellent quality counterfeit money. There were no trained personnel in any government or private corporation who could tell the difference between Cabbage's *cabbage* and the American *dollar bill*. The counterfeit money was truly inconspicuous *cabbage*.

Now Len Cabbage decided that he should have some protection for his small group of counterfeit bandits so he sent ten men to Chicago to buy guns from Gung Ho. They paid for them in cash, of course, with inconspicuous *cabbage*. It was a sizeable order, too, even for John T. Boodle's corporation.

While Cabbage's men were in Chicago, they also made use of the services of J.J. Hooker's division, again paying in inconspicuous *cabbage*. Similarly, certain quantities of drugs were purchased with the same currency. And even though Boodle's staff were well trained to spot *bad boodle*, this *cabbage* was really inconspicuous.

However, when all the weekly funds were lodged with Denny Dinero, he noticed a different texture in the paper among the individual one *dollar* bills. He had his laboratory assistant test the paper of both *dollars* only to find that one was inconspicuous *bad boodle*. John T. Boodle was notified at once, and an executive meeting followed shortly thereafter. They had to determine where the money came from and, more importantly, who created such fine quality counterfeit bills. A committee was formed, headed by Denny Dinero, to investigate the situation and report back to the Executive in one month with their findings and recommendations.

Dinero and two other employees traced the source of the inconspicuous *cabbage* back to Len Cabbage in Los Angeles. There they stayed for fifteen days in a cheap hotel to watch Cabbage's operations. They observed that Cabbage, now having perfected counterfeiting, was branching out to include protectionism, prostitution and drugs – potentially a tremendous threat to the Boodle operation.

In the meantime, the Federal Government noticed the excess currency in circulation and was having difficulty reconciling it with its own *dollars* in circulation. So the government's investigators questioned Boodle for some time concerning the matter. They were convinced John T's corporation was behind the surplus *dollars*, but lacked the proof to lay charges.

After the government investigators had returned to their own offices to review the facts, Denny Dinero returned from Los Angeles with his *cabbage* report. He had concluded that Len Cabbage was building a better, more efficient organization in all the same functional areas as Boodle – Cabbage was becoming an economic threat.

John Boodle was beside himself. Here, he had built an organization which made a number of society members happy:
- the unemployable were employed;
- customers of the prostitution division were satisfied;
- drug users had secured a steady source of supply;
- shopkeepers were protected; and
- the corporation was literally making money.

The only party which was not happy was the government. It was receiving no income tax on the corporation's profits and it had competition for the creation of its money. So Boodle and his vice-presidents concluded that to right the wrong was to have the government happy too. Flowing naturally from this conclusion was the decision to invite the government's investigators to a meeting which was held the next day.

Said John T. Boodle to the chief investigator, "You have been investigating me and my company for a long time. You have found no evidence to support your suspicions but yet you continue to harass me and my people. Why do you do this when our company has made so many people happy?"

"Because," stated the inspector with authority, "you have earned your money from prostitution, protectionism, drugs, arms sales and counterfeit money. Your money has its roots from evil and, therefore, cannot be said to make people happy."

"But is it not true that we have organized the unemployable and given them jobs – and this has reduced the amounts of *dole* you have had to pay?" queried Boodle.

"Yes. And haven't we organized prostitution in one location so it is not a public nuisance on the street?"

"And haven't we protected the shopkeepers which reduces the pressure on police forces to hire more people, otherwise increasing their deficits?"

"And, haven't we localized the drug trade to a point where it is easier for you to monitor it?"

"Yes, yes," sighed the inspector, "but what has all this got to do with the cleanliness of your money?"

"The point is that we have provided a great social service to the government, reducing its cost of *dole* and law enforcement, as well as making those activities it wishes to monitor easier to do so. You owe us a great debt, sir," exclaimed Boodle.

"I see your point, Mr. Boodle, but you have created *bad boodle* and not paid income tax," argued the inspector.

"Was it *bad boodle* now, or inconspicuous *cabbage* that you were referring to?" questioned Boodle.

The inspector produced the *counterfeit dollar bill* which John T. Boodle examined.

"This is too good a copy to be *bad boodle*," exclaimed John. "It must be inconspicuous *cabbage*."

"This counterfeit bill is conspicuous enough for us – we recognized it," said the Inspector.

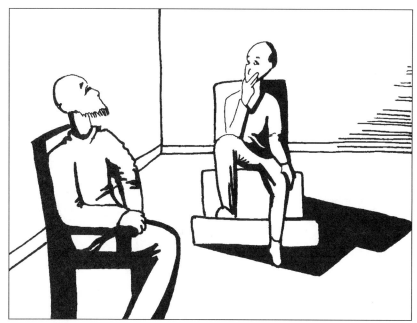

Government inspector agrees with John Boodle that the employment of unemployable reduces dole*, enforcers reduce the requirement for additional policemen, and that having prostitution and drug trafficking in one place is easier for the government to monitor*

"Ah then, you must be right," smiled Boodle. "It is *conspicuous cabbage*."

"What is *conspicuous cabbage*?" asked the Inspector.

"Well, sir, before I answer that, it seems appropriate for us to agree on a few things," suggested John T. "First, can you reconsider, in light of what I have told you, that our business has at least some social value to a number of people?"

"Yes," conceded the inspector, "I can see a certain amount of that, especially if we were forced to raise additional tax money to pay for more *dole* and police protection in your absence."

"Okay then, would it not be logical to assume that the public would think of a tax increase as an evil?" queried Boodle.

"Ah, there is no question about that, sir," agreed the inspector.

"Okay. We agree on everything so far then," stated John Boodle triumphantly.

"Yes, that is fair," consented the Inspector.

"Then, my friend, I put it to you – that if tax is considered by the people to be an evil, and taxes are levied by government, the government, and not money, must be *the root of all evil*! Our customers are happy to pay money because they receive pleasure in return! But I have never known anyone to receive pleasure from paying a tax."

"Your logic is well stated, sir," conceded the inspector, "and we could tolerate almost all your selling of pleasure except for this counterfeit money. It can damage the entire country's economic progress."

"Will you then permit us to carry on quiet enjoyment of our business in exchange for the elimination of those responsible for this counterfeit money?" asked John T.

"Yes!" consented the inspector after some thought.

"Then, it is agreed. Mr. Dinero will supply you with all our information on a Mr. Leonard Cabbage of Los Angeles. He is your man. When you arrest him you will find the counterfeit money which will convict him – his money will be *the root of your happiness*."

"I am much obliged," stated the inspector as they shook hands.

When the inspector left, John Boodle turned toward Denny Dinero, looking pensive.

"You know Denny," he reflected, "when the good inspector eliminates Len and his *conspicuous cabbage*, he will be eliminating our major competition and chief source of aggravation. We will be able to once again freely provide our clients with good service – make them happy to pay money, which makes us happy. And now, even the government has found happiness in money."

$ $ $ $ $ $ $

With John T. Boodle's wealth redistribution plan well into country-wide effect by 1910, all Americans seemed to prosper. The automobile had already been invented, and with its mass production the balance of the unemployed found jobs. The ease of travel by train and automobile advanced communications. Newspapers, and then radio grew into big businesses which, in turn, gobbled up new immigrants standing in the unemployment lines.

Wealth grew faster and in larger amounts than in Europe. And with that wealth came power – both political and economic. But the United States didn't seem interested in world politics at the time. The people were focused too much on internal spending – building homes, buying automobiles and taking holidays – in other words, the American dream. Thousands of people moved from Europe on nothing more than this dream – to have a bright future and to make enough money to live well beyond their *basic bread*.

Politics had matured with Washington's Constitution holding up nicely to world change. The Republican party, which had originated during Harper Shielding's days in Ireland, became strong with its main opposition being that of the Social Democrats. And as the country grew, so did the government and its requirement for *moullah*. It spent money as carelessly as did the people, altogether placing enormous inflationary effects on the nation's economy.

As far as anyone could fathom, there were three sources of the inflationary problem:
- government taxes and corresponding spending;
- full employment with respectable industries, and resulting high disposable income;
- full employment with John T. Boodle's organized crime corporation, and the resulting high disposable income.

Then came World War I which placed additional pressure on the governments of all developed nations. Canada passed legislation in 1914 to establish a one-time income tax to pay for its contribution to the war. And it must have been a very expensive war as that tax still exists. All other countries just increased their existing taxes.

By 1918, the warring nations had racked up tremendous national debts, but continued their spending and taxing of the everyday working man. An example of the stress on the average American, for instance, could be seen in the life of Tex Roll (1885 – 1930), a Texas civil servant.

Tex Roll was responsible for the road maintenance in rural Texas from 1915 until his death in 1930. He listed the names of all property owners on the State 'tax roll' for the purpose of raising taxes to repair roads. He accepted the position only because he had to raise money personally to pay off his debts incurred while attending the State Road School, where he graduated with honours as a Road's Scholar. So, with *basic bread*, a loan payment and his own tax, Tex Roll's life was a financial struggle. In addition to this, he had to endure abuse from the people when he visited them on tax collection day. And even though Tex was the best State budget and cost control manager, on occasion a freak sleet and hail storm would cause unforeseen destruction to the roads. In such cases, Tex would have to go back to the people to raise a *slush fund* to clear the roads.

He was like many over-taxed people throughout the developed world; he could never hope to paddle his way out of the economic backwater. The lack of money both to him and the nation seemed to be the constant source of fiscal misery.

$ $ $ $ $ $

By the early 1920's, people were spending all their incomes without any regard to savings. And, as it appeared that prosperity would always continue and incomes were increasing, an old disease set in – hyper-borrowing. People began to borrow money to buy consumable products and to invest – shades of Governor General Light.

The fashionable thing then was to own shares in companies – to trade on the New York Stock Exchange. Yes, New York had seen fashion change from Trinity Church to pubs to stock exchanges, all in a little more than two hundred years. But the stock fad was different. The people were gambling with money they didn't have, and at the time there were no regulations in place to protect the investor. As a result, people during the 1920's were staring at an economic time-bomb!

The lack of any stock regulations meant that anyone could register a public company and sell shares. And the only information a potential shareholder had was that given to him by an unregulated company. There was no check or balance in the system.

This was an irresistible opportunity for The Boodle Corporation, headquartered in Chicago. Its founder John T. Boodle was now dead and Denny Dinero was President.

Dinero's religious pursuit of money attracted him to the New York Stock Exchange and its ripe opportunities. He wasn't interested, however, in commodities – particularly in pork belly futures. But Denny Dinero was interested in developing a scheme to sell stock in exchange for *moullah*.

The Boodle Corporation owned a subsidiary mining company, The Solid Gold Investment Company, or just 'G.I.C.' as it was referred to within the company. It owned two gold mines in the Midwestern United States, which had been boarded in for the past fifty years. Denny ordered the boards removed and a crew of men

The first stock scam resulted in shares in a worthless mining company being sold for $150 each by The Boodle Corporation

out to each mine to commence digging. News of the digging got around the investment world through certain untraceable leaks. Soon a number of people were inquiring whether they could invest in GIC's shares. Investors were so anxious to acquire a piece of this company, they were offering The Boodle Corporation as much as $100 for each share, which had an actual worth of less than $1.

In the end, Denny acquired and listed the one million shares on the New York Stock Exchange at $150 each. And all were sold within thirty days at the asking price, netting approximately $140,000,000 after expenses. But thirty days after Denny Dinero received his money, the men stopped working at the mines. The shareholders now owned two non-producing mines, shafts and all! The scam was reported to all in authority, but no legislation existed providing authority to act. Dinero got away with the scam money which would forever bear his name – *dinero*.

There were many *dinero* coups on the stock market which resulted in banks demanding payment on most investment loans by 1929. Then the loans, taxes, exorbitant life styles, national debt, and finally the farmers' poor harvest results of 1929, brought the world of money circulation to a grinding halt.

People just stopped spending and when they did, businesses could no longer sell. And when businesses could no longer sell, they lost money. Loans were called and people were laid off by the hundreds, the net effect of which was to ratchet the economy down to the point where people could barely afford their *basic bread*. Farmers, with the drought, could not even grow their own *basic bread*, and when they did, the yield of small potatoes yielded a market price of similar quantity. Hence, the term *small potatoes* for money earned during lean crop years.

Throughout the 1930's, all sources of wealth, on a worldwide basis, diminished substantially. The lack of money caused hardship for families of all nationalities. The socialist and communist backed countries were no different. In fact, they were financially worse off because their economies were usually supported by only one pillar – government. At least the industrialized countries had spread their risk among corporations, government and the people.

In countries such as Russia and China, communism gained a strong foothold based upon the theory it would be the government of the working class, by the working class, without the exploitation associated with capitalism. But unfortunately, what appeared to be sound in theory did not work in reality, particularly when the expectation was for uniform government behaviour.

Both these countries were vast in geographical size – too vast for a government-based economy to develop transportation, communication and, hence, any sort of efficient economic activity. Therefore, economic cushions, financial safeguards or wealth didn't even exist during good times. The people were fragmented and focused only on their own villages and towns. There was no free press to educate them on how extreme their poverty was, and because of this they had nothing with which to compare their own lack of progress.

In addition, the poverty of the communist countries had left them back in the eighteenth century financially, with incomes at less than the *basic bread* level. Many lived from the land while others worked in government factories for *chicken feed*. No matter what the individual circumstances, the family income usually didn't even amount to *small potatoes*.

The net effect of all this was that the depression, which began with the stock market crash during 1929, didn't make much difference to people in these countries. Life continued pretty much as it had during the past number of centuries – people continued to starve. No great amounts of wealth were gathered and then lost during the depression. And so, to these people, the lack of money during the 1930's did not cause a lot of grief and misery – it was something they never had in the first place. That's right. The lack of money in Russia and China up to 1929 was their *root of all happiness* during the 1930's!

$ $ $ $ $ $ $

During the depression, even The Boodle Corporation faced difficult times. Because unemployment was so high, large numbers of people sought jobs with the company. It became difficult to bankroll its payroll. Moreover, people were not buying drugs and prostitutes at the same rate as they used to do.

The vast unemployment also gave rise to rival gangs competing for the same pleasurable *dollar*. Tension rose among these gangs, eventually leading to gang warfare. The lack of money in America had, indeed, led to unhappiness.

These gang wars were, to some extent, an economic godsend for The Boodle Corporation. Arms sales boomed, relieving money pressure created from declining sales in other areas.

However, slight changes were required in the company's strategic plan if it was to survive the depression. One change was a procedural one – that was to refit the protection group to become an enforcement group. Since the shopkeepers were no longer wealthy or as free with their money, it became difficult to extract the normal protection fees. The corporation now had to use mild encouragement on its clients to maintain revenue levels, all of course with the help of the arm's division. Yes, that's right. The protectionist group had now become the reason for its original existence – it was a threat to the shopkeepers against which they, in turn, required protection. The lack of money surely generated confusing behaviour!

This change, however, still did not generate enough money for the giant Boodle Corporation to meet its payroll. The company had to be more creative with its financing. The now aging Denny Dinero called a meeting of his younger executives to discuss the problem. One vice-president asked about the corporate history concerning Dinero's original *bad boodle* group – why had it been disbanded? Dinero explained that the group was eliminated as part of an agreement between John T. Boodle V and the Federal Government – it was the price the company paid to eliminate its then only competition, Leonard Cabbage.

"Well," said the young executive, "it is now 1935 and the Federal Government has no fiscal policy to destroy. Although we are short of cash, we are still operating with strength and stand strong for all the ideal American corporation believes in. We must preserve the American corporate dream. After all, our organization is larger than General Motors. We must 'bite the bullet' and do what is necessary to preserve the entrepreneurial heart of America."

"Well said, young man," spouted Denny, "whatever it was you said. What are your proposing?"

"I propose that we dust off our counterfeit division and manufacture a little *conspicuous cabbage*. But if we do, it has to be used more discreetly and wisely than in the old days. We don't want to attract any attention to this policy change – sort of reminiscent of the management style of the late Lo Ki."

"How can this activity be discreetly executed?" queried Dinero.

"Well," said the young executive confidently, "I propose that we set up a chain of legitimate businesses."

"What?" yelled Dinero. "Go legitimate? That's preposterous!"

"No, no. Please hear me out," pleaded the young man. "We will use the *conspicuous cabbage* to buy land and build small stores across the country. The people are down to their *basic bread*, so I propose we stick to businesses catering to the necessities of life such as bakeries and laundromats. That way, all our capital investment will be made with *conspicuous cabbage* or *bad boodle* and the businesses will be free to operate with legal government tender. They will buy goods and services with real *dollars* and sell their products and services for real *dollars*. We will make a huge profit because there is no real capital investment. It comes from a 'one-time' issue of *conspicuous cabbage*. In addition to all this, we could deploy some of our not-so-busy people to run the operations."

"For added protection, I suggest that we build the laundromats first. We will then launder the counterfeit money through these establishments, but we won't make any *dough* until we build the bakery chain."

"By God, I like it!" said Denny Dinero as his fist hit the table. "Let's do it!"

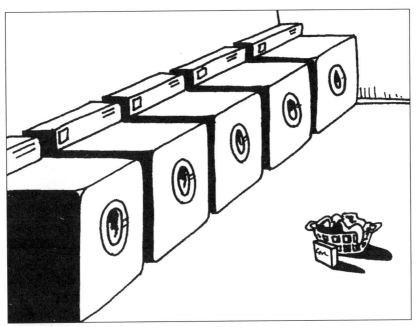

America's first money laundering establishment

And so the counterfeit division was opened with the help of minting plates stolen from and replaced back with the Federal Treasury – just as Leonard Cabbage had done many years earlier. They minted ten million *dollars* which was used to buy land and construct buildings. The company's payroll was paid as well because its men were employed at the construction sites.

Once the company's twenty new laundromats were built, the ten million *dollars* had lost its identity, so more than clothes had been laundered. The Boodle Corporation now had ten million *dollars* of real estate on its financial statements, free and clear of any debt.

The vice-president of finance then mortgaged the properties for seven million real *dollars* and built twenty-five new bakeries which, in turn, became very successful at making *dough*.

But during 1938, at the age of eighty-six, Denny Dinero became ill. And before he died, he sent for the young executive who had singlehandedly pulled the company through the depression. As the young executive stood before Dinero's death bed, the old man said to him:

"I have much to be grateful to you for, young man. Your financial genius pulled the company through the roughest financial times this country has seen. But we are profitable once again, and as you once said, we stand for all there is to the American dream. Your scheme to launder money to make *dough* was so clean that I, Denny Dinero, will die not being able to tell the difference between *conspicuous cabbage* and *bad boodle.*"

8

Current *Currency*

Money was scarce to the everyday person all through the 1930's. The governments tried several methods to 'kickstart' the economies of the world, but without success. The supply of goods and services had not developed because there was no demand – there was no demand because the population was largely unemployed, and people were unemployed because companies were not supplying more goods and services. The governments of the day could not seem to get their minds around this circle.

Then came unlikely economic allies – Germany and Japan. When these two countries instigated World War II, they in effect 'kickstarted' the economies of all other countries. The war took everyone's mind off the depression. There was now a common cause, a united front against Germany and Japan.

The developed-world government allies needed supplies, equipment, guns, aeroplanes, battleships and vehicles – all at once, and in numbers never before seen. All major production plants in the free world were now operating to capacity. Men and women alike were hired by factories to manufacture supplies for the war. Those who were not hired enlisted in the forces to fight and were paid *moullah* by their own governments – full employment was approaching the free world by 1941. Telecommunications had to be improved – the troops had to be clothed and fed; espionage had to be planned; all the while some internal workings had to be maintained in each allied country. That's right. Germany and Japan, by beginning a war with the rest of the world, committed an economic stroke of genius. Or did they?

During past wars, tremendous inflationary problems were created. Usually when governments wanted to finance wars they just printed more money. And the more money in circulation the less valuable it became – business and labour demanded more of it because it was worth less.

World War II was no different. After all, governments were just as poor during the depression as were businesses and the people. So the only way they could afford all this war activity was to follow Denny Dinero's understanding of the American dream – print *conspicuous cabbage*. That's right. The governments had to counterfeit their own currencies to solve the problem. The Boodle Corporation had provided the model several years earlier. And instead of laundering their excess currency through laundromats and bakeries, the governments used their armies, navies and air forces. The principle was the same – they spent their way out of the depression by borrowing or printing more money.

So the Germans and Japanese were a mixed economic blessing for the time. They removed the depression from the people of the free world and placed it square on the backs of the *current currency*. And in the case of the United States these were *greenbacks*.

On balance though, Germany and Japan were the best economic allies for the world because:

- they forced the rapid growth in demand for goods and services for all other countries;
- they provided a psychological focus for all other nationalities to turn to, to relieve the malaise associated with the depression;
- the war revealed how antiquated the world's electronic communications and armed forces equipment really was and, hence, encouraged a great amount of research and development. This gave way to the development of, and investment in, positive consumer products such as computers, jet engines and electronic components;
- during the war all countries realized their strategic defence weaknesses which resulted in additional money being spent on armed forces postwar improvement;
- the deployment of the atom bombs over Japan escalated the demand for money for weapons research to a new and horrific height. Although the use of the weapon was horrific, the money spent within world economies was healthy;

- when Japan and Germany lost the war, the rebuilding of the two countries required the continued employment of vast numbers of people and equipment. So postwar redevelopment maintained a steady economic pace toward growth and prosperity;
- the postwar dispute between the Allied and Communist bloc countries, over the allocation of the spoils, generated a cold war, requiring heavy spending on intelligence and counter-intelligence which, in turn, meant career opportunities for many people; and,
- all these economic benefits, together with the sheer thrill of winning the war, gave the rest of Europe, North and South America and Australia new economic life which hadn't been felt since the 1500's and 1600's – when the New World began to thrive.

These positive economic factors from World War II had to be balanced with certain negative ones – high inflation and national debts. The inflation problem was controlled through monetary policy or the amount of money in circulation together with the implementation of strong fiscal controls, such as those advocated by John Maynard Keynes.

The national debts were not as great a problem for the time being for two reasons. First, inflation meant the debts would be repaid with money which was worth less than when the money was originally borrowed. And secondly, the economies were growing and prospering which, in turn, generated tax money to help governments eliminate their national debts.

While this economic beehive of activity was going on, the Americans and their allies overlooked a point of historical significance, which came disguised as a welcome relief. The Japanese, through their new constitution, rendered the declaration of war by their country, any time in the future, illegal. To the western world this was pleasing, but to the bright economic mind, it was really the turning point for what had appeared to be a lost war for the Japanese. That one clause in the Japanese Constitution meant they did not have to allocate great amounts of their national budget toward the military. Any future capital created could be completely available for productive and consumable goods and services.

In Europe, the economic restoration of Germany was not conducted as smoothly as it was in Japan. The communists demanded their territorial 'pound of flesh' – which resulted in Poland, Czechoslovakia, Hungary, Romania, Bulgaria, certain Baltic states and half of Germany coming under the Soviet Union domination. The United States rebuilt the western portion of Germany, but the Soviets did little restoration to the East because their system provided little incentive to do so – and the government was then out of funds.

The territorial clash between the Soviet Union and the United States escalated the political paranoia which flavoured the 1950's. In the United States there was 'a communist behind every rock', a political attitude which created solidarity and generated vast amounts of money for armaments.

The armaments race was very profitable for many American corporations and scientists. But there the forces of capitalism generally provided sufficient *basic bread* and *wild wampum* first, so no one noticed any economic day-to-day suffering as a result of the government's massive investment in a dead-end product – weapons.

The Soviets, on the other hand, felt American capitalism was decadent and took advantage of the working class. So, under their system, they diverted funds from the procurement of food and *basic bread* for the working class, to the building of armaments to compete with the Americans.

Under the American system, spending money on armaments created employment and profit during the short term, but a huge national debt in the longer term – all because armaments could only be stockpiled; they could not be retailed to recoup the government's original investment in them. Under the Soviet system, the creation of armaments produced absolutely no economic growth as the manufacturing plants were all owned by the government, and workers received the same state wages regardless of whether one missile or forty were built. And even if they had generated more money for the people, the government's poor allocation system for food, clothing and basic luxuries meant there was no supply of *basic bread* to purchase, with any disposable income. The Soviet system provided no incentive for the people to improve and no goods or services with which to improve. Every available *rouble* was spent on tanks, guns and missiles – an economic timebomb which began ticking for that country after World War II.

So what appeared to be an economic boom for the *dollar* was a complete drain for the *rouble*. The United States knew this. It also knew that no country could ever use nuclear weapons again – at least not without worldwide destruction. So why not fight a different war? Why not bring your enemy to its knees economically? And so United States economic policy became clear for the period from 1970 to 1988. It was not building armaments to use against the Soviet Union, or China for that matter. It was running the ideal economic race, one that strengthened its own businesses and people with money, and, at the same time, weakened its opponents who were trying to maintain the same pace.

The race eventually resulted in the Soviet Union's seeking economic peace with the United States, by offering to reduce nuclear warheads in the name of world peace. While the world looked upon this as a step toward peace and a lessening of international tensions, both countries were really playing the money game.

$ $ $ $ $ $ $

Throughout the period of 1945 to 1975, economic distance grew between the underdeveloped poorer countries in Africa and South America, the communist under-industrialized countries, and the totally free industrialized western world. The latter grew once again in wealth at a great rate. They invested steadily in West Germany and Japan who, because of their high productivity and low labour rates, paid healthy dividends to the developed nations. And because of their economic power, the completely industrialized countries were referred to as the 'First World'; the lesser industrialized Communist bloc countries became the 'Second World'; while the totally helpless and underdeveloped countries were the 'Third World'.

The First World was led primarily by the United States because of its dominant investment in other countries. This dominance, in turn, was the primary reason why the American *dollar* became the international language for money. And with the title of 'universal language of money' for the dollar came the role of world banker for the United States – an awesome responsibility all around, and a long way from the days of Chief Little Dole and the humble beginnings of Wall Street.

With mega-foreign investment by the Americans came a corresponding growth in foreign exchange and money market movements – a system which, in itself, consumed great amounts of money to pay for overhead expenses. So although the American system generated the greatest wealth, the ego of its government and entrepreneurs caused it to accept many expensive world positions – such as:

- military power of the free world by assuming a global protectionist role – the ultimate of John T. Boodle's dreams;
- world banker and controller of monetary policy for the free world; and
- leader in postwar restoration.

As with everything else, there was a price for ego. And the American people were paying this price, not only through taxation but also through loss of money internationally – money which otherwise would have been available to upgrade the plants of America. Money had gone well beyond the level of *basic bread, wild wampum* and *widow's mite*. It had become an international game!

In addition to the noted drains on the American economy and its currency were its attempts to turn the Third World into satellite capitalist countries – made in its own image. The Third World policy of the United States was to throw enough money at a problem so it would disappear, turn into a profit, and everyone would be happy – not the case with the Third World where people didn't even have the basic skills to grow their own food. People in these countries were totally under-educated, unskilled and hungry. They certainly were a long way from understanding the American lifestyle, and the Americans were a long way from understanding Third World problems, much less their different cultures.

So the United States made sovereign loans to the Third World in such magnitudes that borrowing countries could never hope to repay. In addition to these loans, the United States gave grants to help feed the starving peoples of these countries.

The loans and gifts of money were only sufficient to barely operate these Third World countries. It was never enough to assist in any sort of permanent development plan. So, in substance, money, given or loaned to those countries, was really *dole* on an international level. The old Chief would have been proud that his idea had gone this far – and had made this much impact upon the world. But it would have come as no surprise to Chief Little Dole that if *dole* caused problems in New York it would also cause problems in the rest of the world.

Third World countries used their sovereign loans and *dole* to maintain their often dictatorial governments which, in turn, provided less *basic bread* than needed by their people. They became dependent upon *dole* money just to live. No effort was made to become self-sufficient. And because their economic aid was feeding women and children, the United States and other supporting countries could not even consider withdrawal of international *dole*. It had become a vicious economic treadmill upon which the poor people of the earth could never hope to move fast enough to prosper, unless there was sufficient western capital to teach self-sufficiency.

The overall effect of aid, military support, banking and restoration was that excessive amounts of capital left the United States. So, oddly enough, the United States found itself having to borrow from other countries just to continue with its worldly overhead expenses – a humble position for a 'supertanker size ego'. And the logical sources of such borrowed capital were the countries it had restored since World War II – namely, Japan and West Germany.

Japan, by the 1970's, had created the greatest return for the American investment and, therefore, had produced a sizeable surplus of cash for further investment opportunities. Eventually, this money found its way into countries along the Pacific Rim and to the reduction of World War debts. But by 1989, the states were very short of cash, and the United States, as a country, was charging higher-than-average world interest rates on loans to satisfy its own cash shortages.

Now the Japanese not only offered cheap and efficient labour, but also cheap and efficient money – a natural by-product of their hardworking culture. And because interest rates on loans from Wall Street were so high, the individual states in need began to look at world money markets – and lo and behold, the Japanese money was the cheapest to borrow. This was the first individual financial step taken by any of the states. But where money was concerned they always wanted to maximize it at the minimum cost. So, during 1989, the State of Kentucky became among the first states to officially borrow money from Japan – a humiliating act considering the United States had destroyed Japan's economy some forty-four years earlier.

Nevertheless, Kentucky borrowed approximately seventy-eight million *dollars* to create jobs which would, in turn, generate additional state tax, ostensibly to help to repay the Japanese loans – good in theory but not necessarily practical considering the nature of the Americans. They borrowed from tomorrow to spend for today. They certainly could have learned a lesson from the likes of Moses Moullah, Barticus and Governor General Light.

Twenty-eight other states explored the idea of borrowing from Japan during 1989. And, during the 1980's, money was coming from Japan in more than the form of loans. Between 1980 and 1989, almost six hundred Japanese companies began operations in eight states, employing more than fifty-five thousand people. There was heavy investment in real estate to build hotels, as well as Toyota and Nissan automobile plants.

The Japanese were brilliant – they had begun a quiet economic takeover of the most powerful country in the world. Their investment was the beginning of the decline of the American empire. The lack of money, after supporting its inflated world ego, meant the United States could not improve production, plant modernization or employment efficiently at home. American plants fell into decay and some of its cities looked not much different than those in the Third World. And so, by the end of 1990, it had become a *de facto* Third World country economically, carrying on the charade of a 'superpower'. The lack of money was about to cause considerable unhappiness.

$ $ $ $ $ $ $

John Pin (1930 – 95) was an average American who was born and educated in Boston, Massachusetts. He obtained his Engineering Degree in 1951 from M.I.T., and began working for IBM in the computer design department. John stayed with IBM throughout his very successful working career, rising to vice-president before his retirement in 1985.

John married Shirley in 1955 when neither of them had very much *pin money*. But by 1956, John had received a sufficient number of raises from IBM that he could afford to buy a small house with a large mortgage. The family was proud of the house, and its purchase represented progress for them.

They had two sons, Bill and Fred, and the family had a happy life together. As a typical four-person American family, they owned a station wagon, two television sets and took a summer holiday every year in North Carolina. The boys drank cola and went to movies and many high school dances.

As part of his compensation package with IBM, John received stock options at very favourable prices. They were, by no means, a *fast buck*, to coin a biblical phrase, but their value grew steadily throughout John's career. He also received special bonuses whenever he accomplished an award-winning computer design.

When Bill turned sixteen, family transportation was under a great strain. There was basketball practice on Mondays, music on Tuesdays, parent-teacher meetings and business meetings – all of which were too much for one car. So in 1972 they bought the second family car.

With all John's prosperity, he paid his mortgage down by ten per cent each year, and increased the *widow's mite* by ten per cent of his earnings each year. The family wanted for nothing.

When John turned fifty-five years of age, IBM approached him with an early retirement package. He was offered a full pension and a cash settlement of one hundred thousand *dollars* for his handshake with the company – a *golden handshake*, one might say. And being a man in constant pursuit of the *almighty dollar*, he thought he could use the extra *shot in the locker* for his *slush fund*. This brought the total family *slush fund* to $750,000 which, when invested in government bonds, would yield approximately $75,000 a year in addition to his pension. So John Pin, the cautious money manager and descendant of Sir William Pin, accepted the retirement package.

John and Shirley enjoyed their retirement years, and the boys had now graduated from university and entered the workforce. This permitted John and Shirley to spend six months in Florida worry-free every year and six summer months at their Boston home.

John's favourite pastime was reading newspapers in general, and financial sections, specifically. He was pleased to read about the free trade agreement between his country and Canada. Millions of *dollars* in tariffs between the two countries would eventually be removed – probably good for the computer industry, he thought. Millions of *dollars*, he thought. Boy, *that ain't hay*!

Each day John read more about the obsolescence of the American production plants, the poverty in large cities, and the fact there were fewer *dollars* to replace roads, streets and sidewalks. He was very concerned for the future of the United States, especially now that he was reading about the country borrowing from Japan. It was 1989 and his country had to borrow to pay for its *basic bread*! How sound was his own investment in government bonds? Would his retirement funds ever be in jeopardy? What would happen to the average American businessman? John worried.

$ $ $ $ $ $ $

By 1987, the Soviet Union had come to realize it could no longer compete in the arms race at the same rate as it had in the past. Its internal economy was on the verge of collapse, and the then president Gorbachev knew the only possible alternative was to disguise a full-scale reduction of military spending by assuming the leadership for world peace – all to reorganize the country's political structure and allocation of resources. In this way, he appeared to be a hero on the world stage as opposed to the leader of a major power forced to reverse forty-five years of military policy. Even though he had no alternative but to divert military funds to *basic bread*, he had to save face while doing so.

His timing was almost too late. The people were becoming disillusioned with promises of reform and more food supply. Even the country's agricultural expert was calling for radical reform involving American-style incentives for peasant farmers to increase their food output. If this did not happen quickly, the Soviet agricultural expert expected famine within the near future.

One of the country's economists felt that unless the food picture improved within two years, their society would be destabilized and something unpredictable might happen. All could be made right if more money existed and was allocated as *basic bread*. As was the case in America, the lack of money was about to cause considerable unhappiness.

$ $ $ $ $ $

Vladimir Smeernoff (1931 – 96) was a Muscovite engineer with similar training, experience and age as John Pin. He and his wife lived with their two sons in a small apartment in Moscow. The rooms were dimly lit and plainly decorated. On his meagre state salary, Vladimir could not afford an automobile, and even if he could, gasoline was only readily available to government officials. He could never save enough *roubles* to buy a house, except perhaps in the country. But even then he would require government approval to buy such property and such approval was usually obtainable only if one knew someone of power within the government.

Vladimir was a successful state engineer, just as Pin was for private enterprise. Nevertheless, the *wild wampum* portion of his family budget amounted to a bottle of vodka each week. He was given leave from his job for two weeks each year but could ill-afford a vacation. Instead, he worked those two weeks, illegally, in exchange for food. So, generating any *widow's mite* was out of the question for Vladimir Smeernoff.

Vladimir read the Moscow news weekly, but there was little international information available for him to digest. He didn't receive any news which would have permitted him to compare his own personal progress with that of the John Pins of the world. He led a lonely, secluded life with no incentive to improve his social standing. And when Smeernoff finally retired in 1986, he didn't receive a *golden handshake*. He received seventy-five per cent of his already meagre salary and was moved to a lower class retirement accommodation in the country.

So Vladimir, unlike John Pin, wanted for everything. He was one of millions of average Soviets whose discontent was placing pressure on Gorbachev to move closer to some variation of an American theme on capital incentive systems. But would it ever come? Vladimir worried.

$$\$ \$ \$ \$ \$ \$ \$$$

Although the United States and the Soviet Union differed greatly in their ideologies, they both had become states of unrest because of lack of money. And, notwithstanding their ideological differences, their problems seemed to bring them closer together. The Soviets began issuing permits to the Americans to open businesses in Moscow – McDonalds were among the first to do so. Relations warmed throughout the 1990's, beginning with the reduction of nuclear missiles in Europe and a corresponding withdrawal of troops. And in 1995, the two countries negotiated the re-creation of one Germany from the then fifty-year split between East and West. The two countries were to be reunited gradually over a ten year period – a cautionary period to compensate for fifty years growth in cultural and economic differences.

By the year 2000, the Soviet Union had gradually instituted certain financial incentive systems and human rights reforms to the point where it began to resemble a socialist state supported by capitalism. At the same time, the United States, to accommodate the poverty in its country, developed a more socialistic domestic policy. So by 2015, it was difficult to see the once dominant ideological differences between the two countries. They had now embarked upon a joint economic development plan for all Europe which included expanding the European Common Market to include both the old east and west blocs. This achievement finally solved the food supply problem in the Soviet Union as the western countries were producing more food than they could consume themselves.

All this activity, on the part of the United States, was financed largely with Japanese money which was now finding its way to the Soviet bloc countries through American loans. By the year 2015, the Japanese held seventy-five per cent of the United States' national and state debts while, in turn, the United States held approximately sixty-eight per cent of the Soviet bloc debt. Except for those countries under the influence of mainland China, Japan now financially controlled all the countries which had physically destroyed it during 1945 – and without firing a single shot!

Japanese money had now brought happiness to the rest of the world specifically because it:
- corrected the overspending by the United States, on a non-productive international infrastructure;
- provided capital to develop socialism in the United States;
- provided capital to develop capitalism in the Soviet bloc countries; and
- generated an economic atmosphere whereby it was more profitable to reduce the level of world arms and enhance world peace.

The net effect of this chain of events was to place Japan as the 'First World'; the United States, Europe and the Soviet bloc countries as the 'Second World'; and all remaining countries which had become poorer, continued as the 'Third World'. So by 2020, for each one of the one and a half billion people who found Japanese money to be the root of all happiness, there was one group who did not – the penniless!

9

Future *Funds*

Sum Yen sat down beside his grandfather, Li Sum, in their waterfront Tokyo condominium. They had just returned from the express train which had taken them to the other end of Japan for a Sunday picnic. Time spent with his grandfather was treasured by Sum Yen because his grandfather treated him like an adult, instead of a twelve-year-old boy – a relationship which had fostered long fruitful discussions about the world and how it came to be what it was now in 2050. Sum was particularly interested in the world of money and how it came to be – and Japan's position in the world of finance. After all, Sum's own father was a billionaire, so he felt a personal need to know as much about money as possible. Consequently, Li Sum found himself frequently under the fire of Sum's questions, at a rate as rapid as the express train.

"There is so much for me to learn about money, Grandfather – where it came from, how negotiations began and when businesses were developed. Can you summarize what happened in money history for me once again, Grandfather?" spouted Sum Yen.

"I think," replied Li Sum pensively, "that the easiest way would be for me to list certain 'firsts' in the history of money. I knew you would catch me on that question today, so I took the liberty of preparing just such a list," smiled Li Sum, as he handed Sum his June 13, 2050, list of first events involving money.

Sum Yen studied the list closely, and as he did he recognized the names of famous people from his classes in world religion and history. He asked his grandfather a number of questions about each character and their contribution to the development of money.

List of First Events Involving Money
Prepared by Li Sum – June 13, 2050

Person who Founded Event	Invented Event	Approximate Date
1. Abraham	Negotiation	Before time
2. Abraham	Deal reneged	Same time
3. Moses of Moullah	Promissory note or money	Before reality
4. Barticus	Barter	Before Christ
5. Moses of Moullah	Currency collapse	Before money mattered
6. Moses of Moullah	Restoration of wealth	After money mattered
7. God	Landlord	All the time
8. Paul	International money exchange	10
9. Drachmas	Inflation	11
10. Deficitus Expendus	Borrowing money for current expenses	265
11. Augustus	Civil servants	270
12. Fastidious (Buck) Dibs	Theft of money	811
13. Desbois Able	Disposable income	1225
14. Sir William Pin	Pin money	1469
15. Harper Shielding Jr	Republican party	1490
16. John T. Boodle	Piracy	1530
17. Woody Barker, Jack Nimble & Francis the Torturer	A limited company – The Nimble Wood Joint Stock Company	1553
18. Francis the Torturer	Labour negotiations	1557
19. Chief Little Dole	Wild use of disposable income	1653
20. Chief Little Dole	Welfare system	1684
21. Pheneous Midas	Industrial revolution – the production line	1742
22. Pheneous Midas	Pudding engine	1745
23. Pheneous Midas	A monopoly	1746
24. Sir Sebastian Cabbage	Documented substantial bribe	1827
25. John T. Boodle V	Organized crime	1890
26. President of the United States	Continued military build-up for economic gain	1981
27. Leader of the Soviet Union	Military reduction for economic gain	1988
28. Leader of the Soviet Union	Economic ties with U.S.	1989
29. Governor of Kentucky	Borrowed money from Japan	1989
30. United States	Became formal economic colony of Japan	2045

He had difficulty at first understanding how God could be a landlord, and what the significance of *Pin money* was. Then Sum Yen wondered, when he read further down the list, why the President of the United States had called the Soviet Union an 'evil empire' during 1981– 82, and had built vast numbers of weapons in the support of this political position.

Li Sum confirmed this to be his recollection of the history of that time.

"Then, the leader of the Soviet Union made an offer to the United States to reduce its weapons to secure credibility and the confidence of the people of the world?" queried Sum Yen.

"No," responded Li Sum quickly, "he offered to reduce weapons to ease the strain on his country's money so, in turn, it could stop creating weapons to kill while its own people were starving. He made this offer in the name of world peace, as a brilliant political strategy to save face or disgrace."

"But this was the right thing to do because strong economic ties grew from this daring strategy, between these two former arch rivals?" questioned Sum Yen.

"Partly, Sum," said Li. "The world domination by the United States plus the subsequent union and development of Europe was very costly to the Americans. They had to borrow very heavily from us."

"Is that how we acquired so much control of the United States, Grandfather?"

"Yes, the United States ultimately defaulted on its loans and we sent teams of financial experts there to help them, and to recoup some of our money America became sort of an informal economic colony of Japan by 2020, even though formal agreements were not signed until 2045."

"I see, Grandfather, there is a pattern to this history, is there not?" questioned Sum Yen.

"I believe there is," reflected Li Sum. "History seems to show that where there is no money there is a void or unhappiness. Then, man sets out to acquire it. And the act of acquiring money somehow brings happiness in to fill that void. But the void is like your 'sweet tooth'. It becomes larger as continued satisfaction may only be maintained by acquiring more."

"So you see, Sum, man has a history of wanting to surpass his own requirements for money – out of sheer love for the process.

Sum Yen learns of the history of money from his grandfather

In other words, my son, the initial acquisition is for need – larger acquisitions of money are for greed."

"Then what happens, Grandfather?"

"Well, when greed takes the place of need, people, or countries for that matter, become out of control. They are acquiring and spending more money than they require. And, as you might guess Sum, this cycle cannot go on forever. Something usually happens to either reduce amounts of money being acquired or cause too much money to be spent."

"Is this what happened to people like Moses Moullah and the Americans?" asked Sum.

"That's right, Sum. In both cases they experienced too much money in circulation and too high an expenditure level. Eventually their economies collapsed."

"Is that ever likely to happen to Japan, Grandfather?"

"No, Sum, I don't think so. You see, as written in the old Christian Bible, in I Timothy 6:10 – 'for the love of money is the root of all evil'. To the Japanese, son, money itself is the root of all happiness. I read somewhere that the Christian God deliberately did not create money in the eyes of his people. Moses of Moullah invented it later during biblical times. Instead, their God created greed through jealousy, competition, anger and other evils. And with these evils, their God taught men to kill, renege on his word and to be promiscuous. These were man's roots to all evil. We would not be so foolish as to substitute 'love of money' for the true purpose of money itself. To us, only the lack of money is the root of all evil!"

$ $ $ $ $ $ $

By 2050, Japan was the world financial power with the Second World clearly under its control. The entire Third World, on the other hand, was under the continual influence of mainland China – and this included most of Africa, South America and smaller Far Eastern countries.

China and its satellites were really struggling to acquire their *basic bread*. It was not concerned about world finance when its people were starving at a rate of half a million a year. Its main concern was, simply, employment of its people – preferably outside its own country. This type of employment generated *yen* and *dollars* for China which it could then use to purchase oil and gas, and processed goods from the Second World countries through Japan.

The government of China was still a communist one and of a strict dictatorial nature. Basically, that was the only way it had survived its many attempted coups over the years. The Chinese people who were unhappy with their lack of money were scattered all over the country. And with poor communications, as well as government suppression, the unhappy had no hope of uniting their three billion in numbers sufficient to overthrow the government.

The Japanese, on the other hand, had more money than they needed. There was virtually no lower class in Japan and million-aires were as common as cornerstores. Everyone had *wild wampum* and no one wanted for *pin money*! Luxuries were a necessity now to the once hardworking and labour-efficient Japanese. No one in Japan wanted to do menial tasks and, even if they did, their labour rates were greatly inflated.

So Japan, since the year 2020, had gradually hired more and more Chinese labourers from the Chinese Government to complete all Japan's labour intensive tasks. Every job from garbage collection to factory work was now held by the Chinese. And this cheap and more efficient labour rendered the Japanese operations more profitable which they had to be to support all the would-be Japanese labourers now basking in a sun of wealth.

By 2050, there were approximately five million Chinese working in Japan. The arrangement with the Chinese Government was that Japan would pay one billion *yen* per week in exchange for all labour services provided. This was very inexpensive for Japan because its own people would have demanded three times this amount. Besides, investments directly in the United States and indirectly in United Europe and Soviet bloc countries, returned the equivalent of the one billion *yen* to Tokyo on a weekly basis. So the Japanese Government simply set aside its dividends from Second World countries to pay for its Third World labour. All other surplus funds were invested in fixed longer term investments which generated higher yields. And liquidity was not an issue as the country's only external financial commitment was for labour, and that was paid from the weekly transfers from New York, Moscow and Europe.

In Europe, the United States and the Soviet Union had completed three quarters of their redevelopment plans. The new high speed rail transit was now in operation from Vladivostok to London. Free trade among all countries between these two points, formerly the Soviet bloc, Middle East, Western Europe and the British Isles, was now completely phased into the economic infrastructure. Food, clothing, electrical goods and fuel travelled freely among the countries without tariffs or regard for borders.

This gradual unification process began during 1992 with the de-emphasizing of the then continental European borders. Great Britain originally resisted the loss of its influence, primarily because it continued to behave with all the paranoia of a declining empire.

Nevertheless, as time progressed all of Europe consented to a common currency, as well as an automobile licencing, health care, population census and civil service system. And when the Middle East and Soviet bloc countries saw the economies to this scale, they eventually joined.

All the countries were members of the European Common Government which was formed to administer redevelopment and taxation of its people. The common currency, *Eurodollar*, was in use with ease, rendering the old geographical borders less important to the countries. Taxes were levied on all goods and services and allocated pro-rata, based upon population, among the countries. This became the primary source of revenue for the unified European countries as there was now sufficient purchasing power to generate the level of funds necessary to meet their financial obligations to Moscow and New York. The financial world was finally learning that its worth as a whole was more than the sum of its parts.

Now, because all the countries had borrowed heavily from Moscow and New York for the redevelopment of Europe, substantial funds were injected into the European economies. Considerable sums were available to build the express rail, construct new buildings, roads, airport terminals and the like. The extra money in the economies, in turn, employed large numbers of people, all of whom now had greater disposable income. The additional disposable income in the economic system caused a general rise in the level of prices for goods and services – that is, the old historical trend of inflation. And toward the end of the year 2050, inflation was proceeding at the rate of twenty-two per cent throughout Europe. People depleted their savings accounts to 'spend, spend, spend' before prices increased by another twenty-two per cent.

Oddly enough, the governments profited by this erratic financial activity because the goods and services tax was calculated at a percentage of what the people paid for their purchases. So as prices went up, so did taxes. And, since the European Government's obligation to Moscow and New York was in terms of fixed payments, any increase in tax revenue automatically increased their general coffers.

Now this sounded beneficial for everyone, but during the early part of 2051, the consumer had had his love affair with spending – and became concerned with his financial future. With no savings and a twenty-two per cent inflation rate, the consumer couldn't keep up! Also, there was only so much in goods and services which an individual could consume. So, by the spring of 2051, the European consumer began to replenish his savings with as much enthusiasm as he had previously spent them.

Obviously, if the consumer was saving at high rates, he was not spending at high rates. And since the economy at the time was driven by spending, it quickly slowed and fell into depression. Now with an economic depression came more than just hardship for the people. It meant reduced taxes for governments. And when the governments' revenues fell, they invested less back into the economy which, of course, meant fewer jobs – and even less consumer spending.

The downward spiral in the circulation of money came to a crisis on May 26, 2051. Consumer spending, having ground to a halt, did not generate sufficient taxes for the European Common Government to meet its debt payments to Moscow. Europe was in default!

Panic was the mood of the Kremlin on that dark May day in the year 2051. All the Soviets' surplus funds were invested in Europe or in its own infrastructure. So the Soviet Union, in the absence of the payment due to it from Europe, was without funds to make its weekly transfer to the United States. The Soviets were forced to declare themselves in default with the United States!

The United States was in a similar financial position to that of the Soviet Union. It was relying upon the money transferred from the Soviets to meet its own national obligations – principally to Japan. It was May 27, 2051, and the United States could not meet its debt payment to Japan. What was to happen?

$ $ $ $ $ $

Sum Yen had just finished his homework for the next day's world affairs class when he came across his grandfather's *List of First Events Involving Money*, prepared almost one year earlier. His grandfather had passed away the previous fall, and Sum was still feeling the burden of mourning. He had loved his grandfather very much.

His eyes went down the page to the last entry when he remembered his grandfather telling him the Kremlin had defaulted on its debt to the United States in 2045. That was when the Soviets could not pay the Americans the first time, which resulted in the United States not being able to pay on its Japanese debt. And that, in turn, was when a debt restructuring among the countries gave official control of the United States, The European Common Government, and the Soviet bloc to Japan.

Now, thought Sum, the same thing had happened – but this time money was not available to Japan from the entire Second World and all its surplus funds had been reinvested back into those countries in the form of long term bonds. Had his grandfather really been right when he said the Japanese were too clever to repeat the history of money as it had affected every other nationality? Sum Yen worried.

$$\$ \, \$ \, \$ \, \$ \, \$ \, \$$$

On May 28, 2051, the Central Council of the Japanese Government met in Tokyo. The then twenty members discussed the country's liquidity crisis and the most available options to resolve it.

When the United States had defaulted before, prior to 2045, the restructuring of its debt to Japan gave the Japanese access to the United States, Europe and Soviet Union liquidity. Since then, Japan had gradually permitted such surplus liquid funds to be invested into the long term European redevelopment plan. This was to buy more oil and gas, and create greater industrial expansion – hence, more tax revenues. It passed all the economic wisdom tests of the time. But then there was no national obligation by Japan for labour costs, or for any other debt. Japan was the world lender and banker – not a borrower. What had changed since? That was the question the Council had to answer.

After a seven-day conference of the Council, it was concluded that since acquiring the industrialized world as economic colonies, only one major economic structural change had taken place – and that change was within the culture of Japan itself, not with the liquidity of the world.

When the Japanese were poor and their country destroyed one hundred years previously, they had worked hard to rebuild their factories, towns and cities. Their forefathers' greatest strength was their ability and willingness to work hard and efficiently. With this work philosophy, cheaper goods and services were manufactured. Flowing naturally from the Japan's work ethic was the creation of its wealth. And because the remainder of the industrialized world had earned more than its *basic bread*, it felt it had become inefficient and lazy, and it didn't have to work as hard. The world's inefficiencies then were Japan's gain.

"Today," concluded the Council, "the Japanese have suffered the same malaise which others have experienced many years ago. The people have departed from what they used to do best – hard and efficient work."

Japan now rested while it paid others to do what its own people were always most capable of doing – production line work for goods and services. In the Council's seven-day proclamation, it decided that the Japanese people must go back to work for their *basic bread*, that earning their *basic bread* was *the root of their happiness*, while earning just *wild wampum* was unproductive. In fact, it had generated the present evil.

$$ \$ \$ \$ \$ \$ \$ \$ $$

On June 3, 2051, Japan's Prime Minister received a diplomatic note from the Chairman of China. Japan was two weeks in default of its labour payments to China – two billion *yen* in debt! The note demanded payment which Japan obviously could not meet.

Days of negotiations followed which saw the Government of China gain certain economic influence over Japan and its colonies. It was the most horrifying and humiliating of times for the Japanese. Japan had secured economic control over all the industrialized and developing world without considering its own vulnerability to the underdeveloped world – the world with the greatest natural resource: cheap labour in search of only its *basic bread*.

That's right. While Japan was basking in wealth for the sole purpose of creating more wealth, its strongest opposition force, while financially the weakest, had much greater motivation. That motivation was to work hard and better itself economically while earning its own *basic bread*. This was the human drive which, together with the industrial world's ambivalence, resulted in the Third World acquiring control of the First and Second! To the Third World, money, because it fed and clothed its people, was now *the root of all happiness*. To the First and Second Worlds, money, because it could buy their freedom from the Chinese, was also *the root of all happiness*!

Bibliography

"Good News Bible - Today's English Version"
British Usage Edition, 1976

"A World History From Ancient Times to 1760"
By Chester W. New and Charles E. Phillips
Published by: Clarke, Irwin & Company Limited
and J.M. Dent & Sons (Canada) Limited, Canada, 1958

"A Pattern for History"
By Arthur R.M. Lower
Published by: McClelland and Stewart Limited,
Canada, 1978

"The Concise Encyclopedia of World History"
Edited by John Bowle
Published by: Hawthorn Books Inc., New York, 1958

**"Profiles & Portraits of American Presidents and Their
Wives"**
By Margaret Bassett
Published by: The Bond Wheelwright Company, 1969

"The 737 Papers"
By Peter M. Cleveland
Published by: Vantage Press Inc., New York, 1989